INSIDE
THE MINDS
OF
SERIAL
KILLERS

An Hachette UK Company
www.hachette.co.uk

Summersdale Publishers
Part of Octopus Publishing Group Limited
Carmelite House
50 Victoria Embankment
LONDON
EC4Y 0DZ
UK

www.summersdale.com

This FSC® label means that materials and other controlled sources used for the product have been responsibly sourced

The authorized representative in the EEA is Hachette Ireland, 8 Castlecourt Centre, Dublin 15, D15 XTP3, Ireland (email: info@hbgi.ie)

Printed and bound by Clays Ltd, Suffolk, NR35 1ED

ISBN: 978-1-83799-671-1
eISBN: 978-1-83799-672-8

Substantial discounts on bulk quantities of Summersdale books are available to corporations, professional associations and other organizations. For details contact general enquiries: telephone: +44 (0) 1243 771107 or email: enquiries@summersdale.com.

JAMIE KING

INSIDE THE MINDS OF SERIAL KILLERS

A CHILLING DIVE INTO THE MINDS OF MURDERERS

summersdale

DISCLAIMER

CONTENTS

INTRODUCTION

Be warned: this book will chronicle the shocking and chilling exploits of modern history's most infamous and persistent serial killers. It will try to get under their skin and understand what drove them to such extremes of horror. It will also touch upon the appalling suffering they inflicted on those unlucky enough to cross their paths. Think twice before you proceed; this book is not for the faint-hearted.

There are more than eight billion living, breathing, thinking and feeling people in the world today. That's more than eight billion private universes, tailor-made to fit the lived experiences and unfathomable imaginations of multitudes. These realities generally dovetail together well enough for societies to tick along nicely. Some private universes, however, can be warped until they break the bounds of everyday, humdrum rationality. Trauma, paranoia, egotism, fanaticism, a lust for power and a legion of other energetic demons make the human mind their playground.

Most of us live by the golden rule of philosophy: we do unto others as we would have others do unto us. Whether we live in lonely wildernesses or busy cities, the overwhelming majority of us coexist peaceably with our neighbours. Our deepest instincts and darkest urges are held in check by a fine spiderweb we might choose to call "civilization"; its threads of inhibition and shared morality appear delicate but are surprisingly strong.

Strong, that is, unless you're one of a tiny, dangerous, elusive minority of humans that exists in each and every society whose minds burn through those threads of inhibition with terrifying results. The worst of them become serial killers. The term "serial killer" describes an individual who kills three or more people in separate incidents over time. This covers a complex range of pathological horrors, and, while criminal psychologists have worked long and hard to unpick the minds of serial killers, there is much about them that remains mysterious. What is clear, however, is that many of us look at the lives and the crimes of serial killers and find ourselves asking one simple question, over and over again: why? Tackling that question lies at the heart of this book.

What is known is that psychopathy is common among serial killers, a state of mind in which empathy and remorse are muted and egotism and ruthlessness dominate. Others have suffered psychotic breaks, making fact indistinguishable from fiction. Many suffered trauma, abuse and isolation in early life, creating inner ghouls that come to possess them. In the most lurid cases, paraphilia, the sexual fetishization of atypical objects, body parts or situations – up to and including necrophilia – is a jarring expression of the killer's cruelty. In the chapters to come, the common features of serial killers will be teased out of their life stories in a bid to answer that nagging question: why do they do what they do?

For all the messy complexity of the serial-killer mindset, one thing is acutely clear: their exploits fascinate us and have inspired many works of fiction and non-fiction. Whence springs this morbid fascination? Perhaps a thought that

INTRODUCTION

begins "there but for the grace of God go I" gives us a pleasant frisson of fright immediately followed by the consoling notion that we are lucky in direct proportion to the tragedy that has knocked on someone else's door.

Perhaps too many of us are armchair detectives, relishing the challenge of piecing a jigsaw of clues together and not dwelling too much on what exactly those pieces are made of in a real-world murder inquiry. Others might think like an attentive prey species, keen to learn the habits of predators and thereby avoid crossing their paths.

There may be a darker explanation for a few of us, a clue to which can be found in Hollywood serial-killer thrillers. In fiction and sometimes in life, prolific murderers are charismatic to the point where many people – not just their victims – are seduced by their heady mixture of confidence, dominance and insouciance. It is worth pondering the fact that charisma is not necessarily a benign or moral personality trait. Its meaning can include both attractiveness and the power to charm or otherwise instil or compel devotion to malign ends. Some of history's most appalling killers and most destructive dictators have lacked personal charm or basic morality while possessing charisma in abundance.

Be on your guard, then, for we are about to delve into the minds of famously frightening individuals. Never forget that the people you are about to meet were far from common criminals; they could be exceptionally charming, exceptionally manipulative or exceptionally repugnant, but always and above all else they were exceptionally dangerous.

And their successors are out there, somewhere.

CHAPTER ONE:

VISIONARY SERIAL KILLERS

THE MIND OF A VISIONARY KILLER

In a German folk story, a man named Faust finds himself prosperous and respected yet still dissatisfied with life. He becomes convinced that a great ocean of intellectual knowledge and sensual pleasure awaits him if he could only find a way to exceed the everyday constraints of mortal life. The Devil meets Faust at a crossroads and tells him that everything he craves can be his if, and only if, he offers up his soul in exchange. The story continues to resonate and has inspired many artistic works including Cross Road Blues, a seminal 1937 blues record by Robert Johnson, who supposedly traded his soul for musical genius.

The notion of deriving power and guidance from otherworldly or divine sources finds a less lyrical expression in the activities of visionary serial killers. While any serial killer can be considered far from any layperson's definition of "sane", the majority are considered as such for the purposes of criminal law in most jurisdictions. Mission-oriented, hedonistic and power-oriented killers rarely succeed when they attempt a so-called insanity plea at trial; for all that they have complex pathologies, they are wholly aware of what they are doing, and that it is immoral and unlawful. Visionary killers, however, have typically suffered psychotic breaks and thereby become wholly divorced from reality to the point where they can't distinguish right from wrong or fact from fantasy. They wield a dreadful power, too often expressed in lethal chaos, but they pay a severe price to their inner demons.

God or Satan might find themselves as co-accused when visionary serial killers are tried, for such killers typically suffer from vivid delusions that are to them utterly real. When such a killer hears a voice in their head claiming to be a supernatural entity with divine authority, they are powerless to contradict it. Herbert Mullin genuinely believed he had to kill to prevent an apocalyptic earthquake. Ahmad Suradji made a Faustian pact of his own, believing wholeheartedly that murdering 42 women and children and sipping their saliva would grant him magical powers. David Berkowitz had clear instructions to shoot courting couples to death from a demon that assumed the form of a neighbour's dead dog. Richard Chase knew with absolute certainty that he had to consume his victims' blood and organs to stop his own turning to powder.

The utter detachment from reality suffered by visionary killers makes their killings messy, chaotic and random. They often murder at the whim of their inner demons and without regard to their own self-preservation. While this generates abundant forensic evidence, it also presents challenges for those in law enforcement whose job is to find patterns and create profiles. It is tricky to second-guess the chatty demon within a fractured mind.

As you read these chilling tales of visionary murder, allow yourself to ponder this question: throughout human history, how many have killed and tortured because mental illness masqueraded as supernatural guidance? Conversely, how many suffering with severe mental illness might themselves have suffered appalling treatment because of the fear they instilled in others? An ancient proverb holds that one who sups with the Devil should use a long spoon.

PARK MYUNG-SIK: THE CANNIBAL OF SINPO CITY

By the standards of Western societies, the inner life of North Korea is something of a closed book. Since the Korean War ended in a 1953 ceasefire that has yet to progress into a permanent peace settlement, North Korea has remained an isolated, repressive dictatorship whose citizens' lives are tightly restricted.

Yet the story of Park Myung-sik, otherwise known as the Organ Harvester, is so shocking and lurid that it has crossed heavily fortified borders to become known worldwide. Over the course of seven months in 1990, Park is alleged to have killed 12 teenage victims in the coastal city of Sinpo. He was not thought to have harboured any particular animus against those he killed; he simply felt compelled to eat the fresh, raw livers of young people in a bid to cure his own liver of cirrhosis.

Park's killings mark him out as a visionary killer because they were inspired by a powerful, all-consuming delusion seemingly fuelled by desperation and illicit superstition. In 1990, Park was a 39-year-old industrial worker in Sinpo

City in the province of South Hamgyŏng on the coast of the Sea of Japan. He was regarded by his colleagues as shy and ineffectual and is known to have been suffering from cirrhosis, a progressive malady by which healthy liver tissue is gradually replaced by scarring, which ultimately leads to liver failure. Park was being treated by a senior doctor but his condition continued to degenerate and he remained in constant pain. There is a possibility that Park suffered from alcoholism to the point where both his physical and mental health were impaired, but this can't be confirmed.

A colleague whispered to Park that a fortune teller might give him what medical science could not. It is a mark of his desperation that he took this advice to heart; North Korea prohibits religious practices in the broadest sense of that term, and flouting this rule could have dire consequences. Nonetheless, Park secured an introduction to a fortune teller and implored them to tell him how he might cure his decaying liver.

The fortune teller was initially reticent but finally yielded to Park's repeated and desperate entreaties, a decision that would return to haunt them. They recounted an old piece of fortune-telling lore whereby cirrhosis could be cured only if the sufferer ate fresh human liver, ideally from a young, healthy subject. Park took this nugget of wisdom and chewed over it for days before he settled on a plan. It seems that the morality of killing to prolong his own life wasn't an issue that particularly troubled him. Of most concern to him was that, as a weak and unassertive man, the physical stress of hands-on, face-to-face murder might be beyond him.

In April 1990, Park saw an opportunity, overcame his natural timidity and tried his hand at murder. In North Korea at this time, students in their mid- to late teens were deployed to the countryside in the spring to help with sowing crops, and in the autumn to help with the harvest. After a hard day's labour in the fields, the students would be bussed back to communal dormitories to sleep the sleep of the physically exhausted. Late one spring evening, Park sneaked into a dormitory, stifled a student's surprised gasp and stabbed them in the abdomen with a blade. He then made a noisy attempt to drag his victim outside, leaving a slippery slick of blood and disturbing a local stray dog. Park dropped his quarry and ran away to a chorus of barks, screams and shouts. The 15-year-old student died in hospital the following morning.

Much less is known about the rest of Park's murders except that he took to heart the fortune teller's advice on eating liver and he learned much from his first, botched escapade. A few days later, a farmer working his fields found the body of another student; when he glimpsed the sliced, clawed and gnawed remains of the abdomen, he fainted. The same week, the remains of a woman in her twenties were found in a similar condition in Sinpo City.

Throughout the spring, summer and early autumn of 1990, Park killed a further nine victims and left a pall of fear over Sinpo City and its surrounding villages. Residents observed a self-imposed night-time curfew and privately derided the police for their inability to find the killer. It is sometimes alleged that, in police states, internal security services are often well equipped for repression but poorly equipped for detecting and solving any crime other than thoughtcrime.

Park finally came to grief in October 1990. He waylaid a student who'd been mobilized for harvest season but failed to dispatch them quickly and silently. The student escaped and screamed for help, and the street filled with angry, fearful citizens who chased Park down, subdued him and delivered him to the authorities in a beaten and bloody state. Park was interrogated and forced to both confess to his own crimes and implicate the reckless individual who'd inspired him. He was publicly executed by firing squad in 1991, and the fortune teller faced their own bitter reckoning, serving 15 years in a prison camp, then being deported far from home.

How Park came to be so passionately devoted to the idea of murder and selective cannibalism that he was prepared to inflict and experience bloody, visceral horror remains open to speculation. Information flows sluggishly across North Korea's borders and definitive accounts are hard to come by. What does seem certain, however, is that, when Park fell to the bullets of his executioners, his liver was still a lethal mess of scar tissue despite the healthy tissues he'd ripped from young bodies with teeth and blade and then gulped down.

HERBERT MULLIN: PREVENTER OF EARTHQUAKES

Between October 1972 and February 1973, Herbert Mullin murdered 13 people in California, USA. While his crimes meet the definition of serial killing in that he killed three or more individuals in separate incidents over time, he is also defined as a mass murderer, a spree killer and a family annihilator. Mullin is most notorious for his apparently sincere claim that his killings prevented cataclysmic earthquakes. He would maintain that, by causing small-scale tragedies, he had prevented the universe from visiting major tragedies on humanity.

Mullin was born in Salinas, California, in April 1947 and brought up in San Francisco. His father, Martin Mullin, was a stern but caring veteran of the Second World War who told his son war stories and introduced him to firearms. Outwardly, Herbert Mullin was a bright, athletic high achiever: he played college sport to varsity level and studied engineering. Inwardly, however, by his mid- to late teens Mullin was struggling with the beginnings of schizophrenia, referred to at the time as paranoid schizophrenic disorder. His mental state degenerated significantly in 1965 when a close friend, Dean Richardson, was killed in a road accident.

Mullin built shrines to Dean and became obsessed with seeking patterns and meaning in nature. He switched his college major from engineering to philosophy, studied the religions of Southern Asia in his own time and became convinced that Dean had died to fulfil a divine, cosmic plan whose shape couldn't be discerned by most mortals. For several years from 1969, Mullin spent time in various psychiatric facilities. While he was discharged each time on the basis that he posed no risk to himself or others, a consensus emerged that he was suffering from schizophrenia exacerbated by the use of cannabis and LSD.

Schizophrenia is a disorder of the mind whose symptoms can include auditory hallucinations and fixed, delusional beliefs. Mullin appears to have suffered both of these symptoms to extreme degrees, hearing convincing but unreal voices and harbouring irrational beliefs that in concert impelled him to kill. Schizophrenia can express itself through negative symptoms, whereby sufferers withdraw from the world and become apparently emotionless and inert. Unfortunately for his victims, Mullin's schizophrenic symptoms were positive, active and quite possibly intensified by drug use.

It is worth taking a moment to point out that it is rare for schizophrenia to manifest itself in serious violence, and rarer still for it to lead to serial murder. According to a study by the University of Manchester in 2016, in the ten years up to 2014 suspects with a history of schizophrenia and other delusional disorders were responsible for six per cent of all recorded and detected (i.e. solved) murders in England. In any given case, schizophrenia was not the only link in the chain of tragedy, and was usually accompanied by substance abuse and various forms of personal trauma. It is also of note that those affected by schizophrenia and other serious psychiatric conditions were more likely to be victims of violent crime, or to take their own lives, than the average citizen.

It is thus all the more tragic that so much went wrong for Mullin and his victims. In 1972, Mullin had turned 25 and was living with his parents in the Santa Cruz Mountains. With the clarity and excitement of a true visionary killer, he arrived at a dreadful conclusion. The fact that he'd been born on 18 April, which happened to match the day and month in which the San Francisco earthquake had occurred in 1906, was a clear sign from the cosmos. The Vietnam War had maintained a flow of sacrificial blood to placate the cosmos but peace was now on the horizon. Someone had to act and that meant him. As if further evidence were needed, he received a telepathic command from his father to begin killing.

On 13 October 1972, Mullin parked his car by the side of the road, opened the hood and pretended to have engine trouble. A homeless man, 55-year-old Lawrence White, offered to help in exchange for a lift. As White examined the engine, Mullin produced a baseball bat, beat White to death and dragged his body into nearby woodland where it was discovered soon after. Mullin would later claim that White had telepathically asked to be sacrificed.

On 24 October 1972, Mullin heard another command from his father's telepathic voice: he was to make another sacrifice in order to avert disaster and ensure environmental purity. He came across Mary Guilfoyle, a community-college student, offered her a lift and stabbed her while the car was still in motion. He took her body into woodland, where he eviscerated her so that he could drape her intestines from branches and check for pollution.

Mullin's mind was in thrall to powerful delusions but he came to doubt that his father was in fact speaking to him telepathically. On 2 November 1972, he travelled to St Mary's Catholic Church in Los Gatos with a view to seeking divine counsel and taking confession. Tragically, Mullin's inner demons had other ideas; we can't know what the unfortunate Father Henri Tomei actually said, but in Mullin's head he asked to be sacrificed for the greater good. Mullin obliged, beating and stabbing the priest to death.

Mullin's story contains several such moments of tragic irony. Periods of clarity occurred during which previous delusions would evaporate, and then the clouds would roll in again and new, lethal fantasies would rain down. In January 1973, he was rejected from the US Marine Corps when he declined to disclose his criminal record. Around the same time, he stopped taking drugs, believing that they were responsible for everything that was wrong in his life. In Mullin's mind, however, making a clean start meant wreaking revenge upon the childhood friend, Jim Gianera, who had first shared a cannabis joint with him.

Mullin travelled to rural Santa Cruz and initially struggled to find Jim Gianera's cabin until a neighbour, Kathleen Francis, gave him directions. Mullin eventually knocked on Jim's door and asked the no doubt baffled man why he'd introduced him to the drug that had ruined his life. Whatever answer Jim gave was not to Mullin's liking, so Mullin shot his former friend. Fatally wounded, Jim tried to warn his wife, but to no avail: Mullin broke down the bathroom door and killed her too. He then returned to the home of the helpful neighbour, Kathleen

Francis, where he executed her and her two children, nine-year-old David and four-year-old Daemon.

Mullin's bloodthirsty delusions remained active and were seemingly easily provoked. While hiking in Santa Cruz's backwoods, he came across four teenage boys camping illegally but harmlessly. He pretended to be a park ranger and instructed them to leave on the basis that they were polluting the landscape. They were not receptive to the advice, so he executed them all with a .22-calibre handgun and left the scene, taking the boys' .22-calibre rifle with him. Robert Spector, 18, Brian Card, 19, David Oliker, 18, and Mark Dreibelbis, 15, were the latest blood sacrifices to the cosmos. As usual, Mullin would later claim that the boys had all telepathically asked to be killed. So wild and random was Mullin's behaviour at this point, it seems unlikely that a more compliant attitude would have saved them.

The race was nearly run. On 13 February 1972, before the four boys' remains were found, Mullin spotted 72-year-old retired boxer and fishmonger Fred Perez working in his garden. He pulled over, got out of his car, rested the dead boys' .22-calibre rifle across the hood of his car and shot Fred through the heart. A horrified neighbour witnessed the whole incident and minutes later an acquiescent Mullin was stopped and detained by the police.

Mullin's career as a serial killer lasted only four months. But for the fact that his final crime was witnessed and a police officer responded promptly and courageously, it might have gone on far longer. When law enforcement hunt down serial killers, they depend on patterns and predictability; many such killers target specific types of victim and use characteristic modi operandi. From this point of view, Mullin's murders appeared motiveless and chaotic, and the police's job would be further complicated by the fact that a number of serial killer Edmund Kemper's crimes (see Chapter Three) were committed in a similar area and time frame.

Mullin openly admitted his crimes, so the only issue in contention at trial was whether he was sane in law. Legal systems around the world vary in their approach to mental incapacity as a criminal defence and the debate surrounding the issue is complex. One possible defence is diminished responsibility, whereby an otherwise sane person can suffer a spontaneous loss of control to the point where specific criminal intent is temporarily in doubt. Another is insanity, whereby a defendant's mental state is so far beyond reason or control that they aren't capable of legal and moral responsibility. The jury in Mullin's case appeared to split the difference: he was convicted of the first-degree murder of Jim Gianera and Kathleen Francis because he'd shown clear premeditation, and of second-degree murder of the rest of his victims because he'd acted impulsively. Mullin died in 2022 after 50 years of incarceration.

Mullin's story could be read as a dark parable of the counterculture. Mullin's father was defined by his military background and patriotism and Mullin himself seemed, superficially, to have been cut from the same star-spangled cloth: he studied engineering, was a varsity athlete and considered a military career. The counterculture that gripped the Western world for ten years from the early 1960s was one in a long line of anti-authoritarian movements, distinguished by a sharp contrast between generations. Many children of the post-war baby boom grew up with levels of affluence and leisure time that their Depression-era parents could not have contemplated in their own youth, giving them more leeway to find new directions and explore new ideas.

The counterculture movement was a watershed for social change in Western societies. Attitudes to issues large and small, from sexuality to women's rights and from hairstyles to hat-wearing, changed significantly. The movement also embodied a dizzying range of artistic experimentation and alternative lifestyles and beliefs, often influenced by or explicitly celebrating perception-altering drugs.

When Herbert Mullin turned on, tuned in and dropped out, the combination of profound mental illness and drug abuse had appalling consequences.

DAVID BERKOWITZ: THE SON OF SAM

Between July 1976 and July 1977, David Berkowitz shot dead six people and wounded seven more in New York City. Frightening as his crimes were, they prompted a wave of media-fuelled fear whose impact continued to resonate long after Berkowitz's arrest in August 1977. Berkowitz is better known as the Son of Sam.

The Son of Sam was born Richard David Falco in Brooklyn in 1953 to Elizabeth Broder, whose straitened circumstances and marital breakdown persuaded her to give away her child. The boy was adopted by Pearl and Nathan Berkowitz, moved to the Bronx and became known as David Berkowitz. While his childhood was not abusive, it was disrupted and unhappy, not least due to his being rejected by his birth mother and robbed of his adoptive mother by cancer during his teenage years.

Berkowitz's adoptive parents sent him to a psychotherapist due to misbehaviour including petty theft and fire-starting. Between 1971 and 1974, he served in the US Army, at home and overseas, and became proficient with firearms. He then returned to New York and at the time of his arrest was sorting letters for the US Postal Service.

New York in the mid-1970s was a city in turmoil. The city's economy was stagnant and its authorities ran out of money in 1975, requiring federal assistance just to keep basic services ticking over. Many working-class areas were derelict or heading that way, not helped by entire areas of the South Bronx being burned down by residents and landlords for insurance payouts in the early 1970s. This contributed 250,000 displaced people to the total of 1,000,000 who would abandon the city by the decade's end; New York's population wouldn't return to 1970s levels until the twenty-first century. Crime and with it the fear of crime also increased markedly throughout the 1970s in what became known as Fear City, eventually peaking in the late 1980s and early 1990s.

Fear City was thus the perfect stage for the Son of Sam. In the early hours of 29 July 1976 in the Bronx, 18-year-old Donna Lauria and 19-year-old Jody Valenti were chatting in Jody's car about the evening they'd just enjoyed at a disco. As Donna opened the passenger door to leave, a man emerged from the shadows, withdrew a handgun from a paper bag, crouched, braced and held the gun with both hands in the manner of a competent, trained shooter, and opened fire. Of three rounds fired, one missed, one penetrated Jody's thigh and one took Donna's life before she hit the pavement. Jody would survive and provide a description that matched Berkowitz. Donna's father would offer a similar description of a man he'd seen loitering nearby in a small yellow car.

Both women had been shot with .44-calibre bullets, a large round for a handgun. The figure ".44" refers to the diameter of the bullet in inches. More standard handgun calibres are .22 and .38; many modern police and military handguns use 9mm ammunition, identical in diameter to .38 rounds but typically shorter and lighter. Berkowitz specifically favoured the .44 Special version of the Bulldog double-action revolver. This snub-nosed (short-barrelled) revolver was compact and easy to conceal but required a degree of skill to use accurately. Its heavy calibre also gave it stopping power and high lethality; .44 rounds can stop heavy animals in their tracks and are sometimes used for game hunting. The use of the Bulldog revolver in the Son of Sam murders hasn't impacted the weapon's sales: production is ongoing and at least 500,000 units have been sold to date.

Another shooting occurred on 23 October 1976 in Queens, establishing Berkowitz's modus operandi. A couple, 20-year-old Carl Denaro and 18-year-old Rosemary Keenan, were talking in her car when the windows began to explode around them. She probably saved both of their lives by instantly starting the car and driving away at speed. Later, they realized they'd been shot at and that both were bleeding. Rosemary's injuries were minor but a part of Carl's skull would need to be replaced with metal. Neither victim saw their assailant but .44 bullets were recovered from the car.

From the autumn of 1976 into the spring of 1977, Berkowitz continued to build the Son of Sam's legacy. On 27 November 1976 in Floral Park, 16-year-old Donna DeMasi had just returned from the movies with her 18-year-old friend Joanne Lomino and was chatting on Joanne's doorstep. A man in military clothing appeared, began to ask for directions, then produced a handgun and opened fire. Donna was lucky, suffering a flesh wound to the neck. Joanne was hit in the spine and rendered paraplegic.

On 30 January 1977 in Queens, 26-year-old Christine Freund and 30-year-old John Diel were sitting in John's car, having just seen a movie. In a replay of the attack on Carl Denaro and Rosemary Keenan a few months earlier, glass exploded as bullets punched their way into the car and John Diel drove away in a panic. While he suffered trivial injuries, Christine Freund died of gunshot wounds in hospital soon afterwards.

On 8 March 1977, 20-year-old student Virginia Voskerichian was walking home in Queens when Berkowitz stepped in front of her and raised his gun. She instinctively tried to defend herself with the books she was carrying, but the .44-calibre round lost little of its power as it tore through paper and cardboard to lodge in her head and kill her. Two days later, law enforcement and the city authorities publicly announced that the same .44 Bulldog revolver had been used in several recent shootings, cautioning that the evidence was equivocal.

The response of the city's tabloid newspapers to the police's March 1977 announcement was far from equivocal, however, and Berkowitz's murders drove a surge in circulation figures for both the *New York Post* and the *Daily News*. Besides the usual degree of morbid curiosity that fuels interest in crime stories, there was a feedback loop of fear: the more the citizens found out about the killer on their streets, the more they wanted to know, and New York's tabloid journalists were happy to meet demand in graphic detail. The effects of this detailed coverage were sometimes practical and visible: the stories made it clear that the killer's type was women with long dark hair, inspiring many female New Yorkers to cut or dye their hair or buy wigs.

The stage was set for more horror and Berkowitz didn't wait long before stepping back into the spotlight. In the early hours of 17 April 1977 in the Bronx, he found 20-year-old Alexander Esau and 18-year-old Valentina Suriani together in a car and shot them both in the head. Valentina died in the car and Alexander died in hospital before he could give any evidence.

Berkowitz upped the ante with this double homicide, leaving a famous letter near the couple's bodies.

Written in emphatic block capitals, the letter was addressed to the New York Police Department from the "Son of Sam", taunted the police for their failure to find him and promised that the killings would continue. In around 400 words of lurid and sometimes incomprehensible rambling, it referred to the writer being locked up and beaten by Sam, a blood-drinking entity who commanded him to "go out and kill". It claimed that the writer didn't want to kill any more but had to honour his father.

Details from the first letter were released to the press and the name "Son of Sam" lodged in the public consciousness. On 30 May 1977, Jimmy Breslin of the *Daily News* received a letter purporting to be from the .44 Caliber Killer. Both the language and the artwork surrounding it were more lyrical and sophisticated than the contents of the first letter. The writer claimed to read and enjoy Breslin's column and promised that, even though they'd been quiet for a while, they hadn't gone to sleep. Perhaps, they added, Breslin would be introduced to Sam. Breslin replied in print, sharing excerpts of the letter, urging the killer to surrender and ensuring that more than 1,000,000 copies of that edition were sold.

On 27 June 1977 in Queens, both 20-year-old Salvatore Lupo and 17-year-old Judy Placido were shot in a car during the early hours. Both would survive but had little evidence to offer. That summer, the New York Police Department imposed a dragnet – a comprehensive trawl for criminal activity – across Queens and the Bronx but were wrongfooted again. In the early hours of 31 July 1977, outside the police dragnet in Bath Beach, Brooklyn, 20-year-olds Stacy Moskowitz and Robert

Violante were found kissing in Robert's car by Berkowitz. He shot both in the head, killing Stacy and half blinding Robert.

The summer of Sam was drawing to a close. Queens resident Cacilia Davis happened to see a yellow Ford Galaxie being given a parking ticket close to the scene of the 31 July shooting. She later saw a man coming from the vicinity of the Galaxie who was holding something dark in his hand, fled from him and heard gunshots. When she reported this, the police sifted through tickets issued in the relevant time frame and location. One detective, James Justis, was given the job of interviewing the owner of that yellow Galaxie, one David Berkowitz. He rang the Yonkers police dispatcher to ask them to arrange it. That dispatcher, Wheat Carr, happened to know Berkowitz; he lived near her and had recently shot and wounded a black dog owned by her father, Sam Carr.

On 10 August 1977, police found Berkowitz's yellow Galaxie outside his home complete with murder weapon, ammunition and crime-scene maps. While they waited for search warrants, Berkowitz exited his apartment block and was detained by officers. Accounts vary but the arrest went peacefully and, by some accounts, cheerfully, with Berkowitz introducing himself as "Sam" and adding, "How come it took you such a long time?"

Berkowitz is generally regarded as a visionary killer, even though his taunting of the police and his post-conviction interviews are more contradictory and chaotic than his actual killings. Unlike Herbert Mullin, for example, Berkowitz did not kill impulsively and indiscriminately; instead, he appeared to target a specific category of victim – young women in cars after dark – and to employ a consistent modus operandi. There was also a degree of hedonism to his killing, as he relished the attention drawn by both his murders and his letters.

Post-arrest, he was assessed as schizophrenic but competent to stand trial. He then rejected his defence counsel's advice to plead not guilty by reason of insanity and instead pleaded guilty to all charges. He was sentenced to multiple consecutive 25-year prison terms and will in all likelihood die in prison. Berkowitz is entitled by New York State law to apply for parole every two years but has on numerous occasions declined to seek early release on the basis that he deserves his fate. More recently, he declared himself no risk to society, regardless of which he was denied parole at his most recent hearing in May 2024.

Berkowitz's initial diagnosis of schizophrenia by court-appointed psychiatrists seemed logical given that he'd presented as delusional with auditory hallucinations. In numerous assessments, he believed himself to be possessed by a demon taking the form of his neighbour's dog, Sam, and to have obeyed its audible commands. He later claimed that he'd only pretended to be possessed, and the degree and nature of his mental illness has been debated by the media and by psychiatrists. As he was deemed mentally competent at trial and was convicted and sentenced on that basis, then, even if there were a consensus that his delusions had been a sham, it would not alter his fate. He has reportedly been a model prisoner for decades, counselling other prisoners, embracing religious faith and campaigning against gun violence.

As the Son of Sam and the .44 Caliber Killer, Berkowitz became a personification of the danger of street-level life in an age of high crime and urban decay. Young women and courting couples out after dark would continue to fear that the shadows between the streetlights might at any moment coalesce into an anonymous shooter who would pump .44-calibre bullets through their car doors, windscreens and bodies, shattering the night and their lives.

RICHARD CHASE: THE VAMPIRE OF SACRAMENTO

Between December 1977 and January 1978 in Sacramento, California, USA, Richard Chase murdered six people, drank their blood and ate their remains. Chase was cursed throughout his short life by vivid, devoutly held and utterly delusional beliefs that would ultimately crystallize into a vision of flesh-eating, blood-drinking horror that would have strained the imagination of Hieronymus Bosch.

While truth is always subjective from a philosophical point of view, Chase's vision of reality was so divergent that it is difficult for anyone not touched by his particular psychosis to think their way into his mind. He was one of the most clear-cut examples of a visionary killer: a wretched childhood and adolescence and an acute manifestation of schizophrenia condemned Chase to live in a world formed by horrifying delusion and chaotic but often bloody thoughts and actions.

Chase was born in Santa Clara County, California, in May 1950. His home life was strict and unsettled. Chase's father used regular beatings to maintain discipline and his mother may have struggled with her own mental health; she would accuse her husband of hiding his mistress in the bushes or drugging her to disrupt her sleep, suggesting a degree of delusion. While not universally accepted, the Macdonald triad of behaviour – comprising severe animal cruelty, compulsive fire-starting and persistent bed-wetting beyond the age of five – is a predictor of violent psychopathy. By his fifth birthday, Chase had manifested all three aspects of this model.

By early adolescence, Chase's disturbing tendencies were no longer limited to torturing animals to death and setting fires. He became convinced he was a member of the James–Younger Gang, the famous band of nineteenth-century outlaws led by Jesse and Frank James; it was a source of deep outrage that his mother declined to buy him a cowboy hat. He became dependent on unhealthy quantities of alcohol, marijuana and LSD, which weakened his already tenuous grip on reality. When Chase began dating in his mid-teens, he found that he was impotent and unable to consummate a physical relationship; it would later transpire that he *was* capable of being sexually aroused, but only by lethal violence or post-mortem violation.

The fate of one of Chase's pet cats offers a window into his tortured reasoning. In 1973, after being repeatedly told by physicians that there was nothing physically wrong with him, Chase happened to see a story on television about a cat that had received a range of expensive veterinary procedures. In Chase's mind, his own cat represented the cat on television and, by extension, the injustice of his being deprived of medical help for his imagined ailments. Accounts vary, but one version holds that he killed the cat, confronted his mother with it, ripped open its belly and smeared its blood on his face.

Chase also developed wide-ranging and highly imaginative hypochondria. Delusions included the idea that his pulmonary artery had been stolen, that the bones of his skull were moving of their own accord and that he could diffuse vitamins into his brain by holding fruit to his head. So varied and chaotic were Chase's delusions that it becomes difficult to pick out an overarching theme, with one exception: he became fixated upon blood, both his own and that of other living creatures. In 1975, he was treated in hospital and then in a psychiatric institution after he contracted sepsis in an attempt to inject the blood of a rabbit into his veins. He would tell staff, inter alia, that his blood was being turned to powder and that his mother was poisoning him on behalf of a Nazi gang.

While detained at the Beverly Manor Psychiatric Hospital in Sacramento, Chase continued to kill and drain blood from wildlife with impulsive savagery. He also acquired blood more methodically, stealing syringes and extracting it from unlucky therapy dogs. After treatment with consciousness-altering (psychotropic) drugs, Chase was deemed to be no risk to himself or anyone else and, in 1976, released into his mother's care. Beverly Manor staff would later tell journalists that they had been constrained by the rules to release him, intimating that they still considered him dangerous.

In any case, Chase's mother was not a fit guardian and decided without medical advice to wean him off his medication. Once back to his old self, he turned his apartment into an abattoir for shop-bought pets, consuming the blood and viscera of dogs and cats. Chase was clearly in a downward spiral and, in August 1977, he was arrested on

Native American land near Pyramid Lake, Nevada, drenched in blood and with a bucket of fresh offal in his truck. The blood turned out to be bovine, no charges were proffered and another chance was missed to prevent horror.

On 27 December 1977, Chase fired a .22-calibre bullet into a Sacramento home, fortunately missing the occupant. He had lied about his mental health to acquire the handgun and later claimed that he'd been shooting at threatening voices. In any event, having a firearm made killing and draining dogs somewhat easier, as he could just put a receptacle underneath the entry wound. But dogs were no longer enough, as Chase had been made angry by his mother's refusal to host him over Christmas and was ready to project his rage onto as many humans as necessary.

On 29 December 1977, police were baffled by the random murder of 51-year-old Ambrose Griffin in East Sacramento. He'd been shot dead with a .22 handgun while unloading groceries on his driveway. In early January 1978, several local residents had lucky escapes when Chase entered their homes, on one occasion relieving himself on an infant's bedding, and on another being chased away; these residents had all been spying on him, he later explained.

Chase's descent into Hell still had a little way to go. On 23 January 1978, he was casing East Sacramento houses for an unlocked door. He happened upon the home of Teresa and David Wallin; David was out at work and Teresa, three months pregnant, had left the front door unlocked while she took out the rubbish. Chase followed Teresa into the house and shot her twice in the head with his .22 handgun; police would later find a defensive bullet wound in one of her hands. He then violated and stabbed Teresa's body post-mortem before removing several organs and draining the blood, which he both drank and bathed in. He further degraded Teresa's remains with dog faeces. Chase would spend the rest of that day calmly watching television at home.

Rock bottom was reached on 27 January 1978. Evelyn Miroth, 38 years old, was at home with her six-year-old son, Jason, her 22-month-old nephew, David, and a neighbour, Dan Meredith. The sequence of events is unclear but, by the time Chase had done his worst, Evelyn's house would resemble an abattoir; he himself offered little explanation, claiming that he'd been semi-conscious during the slaughter. It seemed that Dan had been watching the children while Evelyn bathed; he was likely killed first, shot point-blank in the head with Chase's .22 handgun.

Jason ran for his mother; pausing only to execute David, Chase pursued Jason and shot him twice in the head. He then forced his way into the bathroom, killed Evelyn just as he'd killed her family and dragged her into the bedroom. There followed a sequence of horrors beyond imagination. Evelyn's body was repeatedly violated while blood was sucked from slash and stab wounds. Chase stabbed Evelyn's body in such a way that blood pooled in her abdomen, from which it was drained into a bucket.

He then mutilated David's remains, splitting his skull and consuming cerebral matter. At this point, a six-year-old friend of Jason's had a lucky escape. She knocked on the door, hoping that her friend would come out and play. Chase was spooked and fled the house with David's body, stealing Dan's car in the process. At home, he calmly and methodically cannibalized David's remains before dumping what was left at a church.

Chase was methodical in the execution of his murders and degradation but chaotic in his choice of victim and in his indifference to the lurid trail of evidence he was leaving behind. The FBI were called in and published a profile that fitted Chase to a T. A member of the public named him as a close fit, and a background check on the .22-calibre handgun elicited his name and address. Law enforcement found Chase and his apartment drenched in forensic evidence, from the gore on his clothes to the organs in the refrigerator and the caked blood in the food blender.

In May 1979, Chase was found guilty of six counts of murder in the first degree. The jury rejected the idea that he couldn't have mustered the requisite criminal intent by reason of insanity. At a clemency hearing, the trial judge ruled that Chase wasn't legally insane within the context of criminal proceedings and the determination that he would die in the gas chamber stood. Chase's inner demons had other ideas, however. His fellow inmates at San Quentin, many of them hardened killers, found Chase to be a walking, talking offence against nature. They tried to persuade him to kill himself, and it may be that their whispered entreaties formed a choir with the demons in his head. In December 1980, Chase took his own life with an overdose of psychiatric drugs he'd been caching in his mattress.

Richard Chase attracted the lurid nicknames the Sacramento Vampire and Dracula and is remembered as one of history's most ghoulish serial killers. It should give the reader pause that, while Chase showed more than enough premeditation to be sentenced to death within the law, he also walked and drove the streets of Sacramento stinking, hollow-eyed and caked in blood and wouldn't be returned to any kind of institutional care until six lives had been ripped apart.

SACHIKO ETO: THE DRUMSTICK KILLER

Between 1994 and 1995, Sachiko Eto killed six people in her home city of Sukagawa in the Fukushima Prefecture of Japan's main island, Honshu. Sachiko killed her victims with taiko sticks – implements of various sizes intended for traditional Japanese percussion instruments – while presiding over a pseudo-religious cult of which she was the self-appointed leader.

Sachiko is considered a visionary killer because she appears to have wholly believed that she was acting with divine power and authority and that, by beating her victims to the point of death, she was driving out demons. There is an intriguing degree of overlap between the pathology of visionary killers and that of cult leaders. In the case of Sachiko, she exhibited levels of delusion consistent with schizotypal personality disorder – a disorder typified by emotional estrangement and eccentric beliefs – accompanied by egocentrism and psychopathy.

According to *The Spectator* magazine, in 2021 there were as many as 2,000 cults in Japan, a trend that endures for various reasons. Japan's ancient religion, Shinto, is animistic and polytheistic, celebrating numerous spirits in contrast with the one God of Western monotheism. One aspect of this was emperor worship, which was brought to a crashing halt by the Second World War. Since then, numerous minor religious movements have sprung up to fill the vacuum. Most are harmless, ostensibly following Shintoism but giving the lonely and disaffected companionship and purpose. Many are shady without troubling the authorities, laundering cash for organized criminals or helping the well-heeled to avoid tax. A few have been utterly malign, like Aum Shinrikyo, whose adherents carried out a mass-casualty attack with sarin nerve gas on the Tokyo subway system in 1995.

It is therefore not as unusual as it might seem to Western eyes that Sachiko, born in 1947 at the very beginning of Japan's post-war reconstruction, had been drawn to the world of cults. Clearly, however, she sought something more than companionship and tax relief. By the mid-1990s, Sachiko regarded herself as a faith healer and exorcist. In late 1994, Sachiko resolved to beat the devils out of six individuals with the assistance of her daughter, 23-year-old Sachiko Yuko, her 45-year-old husband, Mitsuo Sekine, and 21-year-old cultist and former member of the Japan Self-Defense Forces, Hiroshi Nemoto.

An unknown number of unfortunate believers stayed in Sachiko's home and were routinely beaten with drumsticks in a bid to drive out a mischievous spirit in the form of a fox. After around six months of this treatment, six cult members were dead and one had suffered severe injuries and been hospitalized. Medical staff contacted the Fukushima Prefectural Police, who searched Sachiko's house in July 1995, found six decomposing bodies and arrested Sachiko and her three accomplices. Intriguingly, the hospitalized cultist was also arrested for assault, suggesting that the accomplices, and perhaps the murder victims, had been induced to beat each other.

It later came to light that her cruelty transcended the spiritual, for one of the dead had slept with Sachiko's lover and another had refused to lend Sachiko a hefty sum of money. It was also observed that Sachiko's former husband had disappeared without trace in the early 1990s as she was building her personal cult, although nothing was proved and no charge brought.

Sachiko's lawyers attempted a defence of diminished responsibility, but the remarkably sustained nature of the violence and the considered malevolence underpinning it doomed this gambit to failure. Unusually for a developed nation, Japan retains capital punishment, and the gallows rope defied Sachiko's self-proclaimed powers of resurrection. While her co-conspirators were sentenced to life imprisonment, Sachiko's long campaign of appeals failed in 2008 and she was executed by hanging in September 2012.

AHMAD SURADJI: THE SHAMELESS SHAMAN

Ahmad Suradji murdered up to 42 women and children in Lubuk Pakam, North Sumatra, Indonesia, between 1986 and 1997. Suradji buried his victims waist-deep in the ground as part of a shamanic ritual, after which he would strangle them to death and use their bodily fluids to supposedly boost his magical powers.

Ahmad Suradji was born in 1949 in Pasar Rongkat, North Sumatra, and was the son of a well-regarded cattle breeder. He got into trouble for fighting and petty theft in his teenage years but remained close to his father. By the time Suradji settled down and took up the cattle trade himself, his father had died, leaving him bereft. Suradji also had a lucrative sideline as a shaman or traditional healer. In some regions of Indonesia, and at all levels of education, wealth and social standing, shamans are widely respected and consulted. Some are harmless and well intentioned and some are con artists; one, Ahmad Suradji, was something worse.

From the mid- to late 1980s, Suradji's reputation as a shaman grew, particularly with women and girls who sought magical help to find the love of their life, to make their existing partners more faithful or to find security, beauty and prosperity. Unfortunately, these women and girls weren't communing just with Suradji but also with the imagined voice of his late father. Suradji had been visited in a powerful vision by the old man in 1986 and commanded by him to drink the saliva of precisely 72 dead young women, as a result of which he would become a powerful mystic healer.

Suradji's father had not explicitly commanded him to kill the young women, but, in thrall to delusion, he acted as if he had no choice. It would clearly take an impossibly long time for him to find 72 recently dead subjects and somehow acquire their saliva. He hit upon a modus operandi and repeated it dozens of times. Women or girls who consulted him would sometimes be persuaded to cooperate with a ritual that entailed following Suradji into a sugar-cane field and allowing him to bury them up to the waist. Having thus isolated and immobilized his victims, Suradji would throttle them to death, then suck saliva from their still-warm mouths. Finally, he stripped them naked and buried them completely with their heads pointing towards his house.

Suradji can be regarded as a visionary serial killer because he was motivated by powerful, imperative delusions that may have been indicative of schizophrenia. He appears to have earnestly believed that he was fulfilling the explicit wishes of his dead father, and also that he genuinely possessed magic powers that could be boosted by drinking the saliva of dead women and orienting their bodies to point towards his home.

Suradji's final victim was 21-year-old Sri Dewi. In April 1997, a local rickshaw puller thought it curious that Sri had asked to be taken to see Suradji but had never asked to be picked up. It is uncertain why it took this long for the deluded shaman to be identified as the common denominator in so many disappearances, but finally action was being taken. Within days, Sri's body was found in a shallow grave by local people and the police were called. They found Suradji in possession of Sri's valuables and in interview he confessed all. A total of 42 bodies were exhumed from the sugar-cane field.

Suradji protested his innocence but was convicted of 42 murders in April 1998. Despite his questionable mental capacity and a last-minute appeal by Amnesty International, Suradji was executed by firing squad in 2008. Remarkably, his three wives had supposedly assisted in his murders and helped to conceal the evidence, although they alleged that they'd confessed only under torture. One of Suradji's wives, Tumini, was convicted but her sentence was reduced from death to life imprisonment.

A plan to inter Suradji's remains in a public cemetery was abandoned by the authorities when they discovered that at least 100 relatives of the dead were preparing to disrupt the funeral rites. Perhaps they sought to deny him the respect and dignity that he had denied their loved ones.

JOSEPH KALLINGER: LIKE FATHER, LIKE SON

"Man hands on misery to man. / It deepens like a coastal shelf." So wrote British poet Philip Larkin in "This Be the Verse". It is hard to find a more lurid example of this notion than in the story of Joseph Kallinger, who survived an unimaginably horrific childhood only to visit that horror on new victims in new ways. Between July 1974 and January 1975, Kallinger murdered three individuals and tortured four family groups, committing most, if not all, of these crimes with his 12-year-old son, Michael.

Kallinger was born in Philadelphia, USA, in 1935 and placed in foster care as an infant when his father abandoned his mother. In 1939, he had the fateful misfortune to be adopted by Stephen and Anna Kallinger, who had a predilection for sustained and inventive child abuse. At home, he was whipped, periodically starved, forced to consume faeces, locked inside confined spaces, burned with a hot iron and made to kneel on sharp stones. There was no escape from misery outside the home: on at least one occasion, he was sexually abused by a neighbourhood gang.

It is unsurprising that Kallinger fared poorly at school and was keen to leave home as soon as possible. At the age of 15, he began to date one Hilda Bergman and, despite the objections of his adoptive parents, they soon married and had two children. While it made sense that Kallinger was eager to escape his childhood home, he would utterly fail to escape the damage Stephen and Anna Kallinger had done to his psyche. Hilda divorced him in the mid-1950s due to persistent domestic violence, suggesting that he was at the very least enacting abuse inflicted on him, or that it had become for him a normalized way of conducting adult relationships. All of this was true and worse besides.

Kallinger remarried in 1958 and had five children with his second wife, all of whom suffered re-enactments of the appalling things done to him in his childhood. He was also institutionalized in both the 1950s and 1960s for various psychiatric crises that had manifested in arson, suicide attempts and amnesia. In an echo of the story of Fred and Rose West in the UK, Kallinger was arrested for violence against his children in 1972 but the prosecution failed when the children declined to testify. Around this time, he was diagnosed with schizophrenia.

In the summer of 1974, Kallinger claimed to be hearing commands from divine voices to undertake actions that would bring on Armageddon and cleanse the Earth of humankind. On 7 July, a Puerto Rican child, Jose Collazo, was found murdered and sexually mutilated in a Philadelphia playground. On 9 August, Joseph Kallinger Jr, one of the children who'd complained to the police about his father several years earlier, was found drowned in a derelict industrial building. Kallinger had taken out a life insurance policy for Joseph Jr two months earlier and claimed that his son had absconded from home. The insurer suspected malfeasance and refused to pay.

During a six-week period beginning in November 1974, Kallinger and his 12-year-old son, Michael, began a campaign of horror across Pennsylvania, Maryland and New Jersey. Their modus operandi was to gain entrance to respectable homes by pretending to be salespeople, after which they would produce knives and handguns and subdue, beat, rob and sexually abuse families.

The Kallingers' spree reached its nadir in January 1975 at a home in Leonia, New Jersey. They initially found three residents, who were made to strip and then bound with electrical cord. Other people happened to arrive at the address and were subjected to the same treatment, the entire ordeal lasting hours. Last to arrive was Maria Fasching, 21, a nurse who'd stopped by to help an elderly, bed-bound resident. She bravely refused to obey Kallinger's degrading orders and was stabbed to death. In the ensuing panic, one of the residents slipped their bonds, escaped and raised the alarm. The Kallingers fled by city bus, dumping their weapons and bloodstained clothing en route.

As is often the case with visionary killers, while the lack of a coherent rationale can initially stymie an investigation, once a pattern does emerge, then their careless and chaotic approach tends to leave a vivid trail of evidence. The bloody, discarded clothing together with abundant eyewitness evidence and Kallinger's well-documented history of violence and mental illness led to swift arrests.

Kallinger's defence team pleaded not guilty by reason of insanity, insisting that he'd acted on God's specific instructions, at least in his own mind. While there is little doubt that Kallinger was profoundly psychiatrically damaged, with afflictions including schizophrenia, it is also the case that insanity pleas rarely succeed. In general, such a plea must satisfy the jury that a defendant was incapable of controlling their own actions, or, failing which, incapable of knowing right from wrong, and consequently could not have formed murderous intent. The sustained, repeated and premeditated nature of the violence in Kallinger's case made this, at best, a tangled ethical web for a jury and so it proved. His first trial in June 1975 resulted in a hung jury, but he was convicted on retrial later that year and jailed for life.

Joseph Kallinger died in prison in 1996. Michael Kallinger was deemed to have been under his father's control at the time of the murders and therefore not acting with agency. He is believed to have been detained at a youth facility until his early twenties, after which he moved to another state with a new name. It is to be hoped that in his case, at least, father did not hand on horror to son.

RAMAN RAGHAV: THE INDIAN RIPPER

Raman Raghav murdered dozens of individuals in India's western peninsular state of Maharashtra between 1965 and 1968. He was nicknamed India's Jack the Ripper due to the almost supernatural dread he brought to the streets of Mumbai. Raghav's killings came in two waves, the first between 1965 and 1966 and the second in 1968. The degree of delusion, the chaotic nature of his killings and the fact that he preyed on those who were itinerant and on low incomes made it difficult to arrive at a clear and complete tally of his murders.

Raghav is believed to have been born in 1929 in Tirunelveli in India's most southerly state, Tamil Nadu. Little is known about his background except that he had very little education and had probably been homeless for much of his life. To compound his misfortune, he was also in thrall to severe mental illness manifesting in powerful delusions that would bring yet more tragedy to those living below India's poverty line.

In 1965 and 1966, numerous motiveless attacks were inflicted on homeless people sleeping on the streets or in improvised shanties in Mumbai's eastern suburbs. Victims were bludgeoned savagely as they slept, with no obvious attempt at robbery, theft or sexual assault. At least nine of the known attacks were fatal. There was a hiatus in 1967 and the lethal attacks resumed in the summer of 1968, again in the suburbs of Mumbai.

As a young police officer, Ramakant Kulkarni was given the daunting task of investigating this case. As recounted by the BBC in 2015, these crimes were initially baffling because they lacked an intelligible motive; the possibility that the assailant had stolen items of low value from victims experiencing extreme poverty could not be ruled out, but even so the extremity of the violence was wildly disproportionate.

Raman Raghav was known to local police and had served prison time for robbery in the past. He had also been arrested during the 1965–1966 murder spree after being seen lurking near crime scenes. Back then, there was no evidence to recommend him as a suspect, but that changed in 1968. One of Ramakant Kulkarni's team, Alex Fialho, remembered Raghav from the earlier inquiry and noted similarities between descriptions given by survivors and suspect photographs from a few years earlier.

Alex Fialho found two plucky witnesses and together they found and detained Raman Raghav. When he was arrested, his clothes were abundantly stained with blood. When interviewed by detectives, Raghav refused to speak and stayed silent for two days. Then, in a moment of inspiration, an officer found the key that would unlock their suspect's mind: chicken. Raghav was asked if he wanted something and he asked for a chicken dinner closely followed by another one. He then asked for a sex worker but accepted that this was not a realistic option and accepted a comb, a mirror and some hair oil as a reasonable substitute. Raghav saw the process as transactional: if the police gave him what he wanted, he would reciprocate.

Raghav certainly did reciprocate, sharing his secrets with detectives, psychiatrists and lawyers, abundantly and at length. He showed them where he had stashed his kill kit, which included a distinctive crowbar shaped like the number seven and various knives. He confessed to committing the 41 murders, mainly in Mumbai's suburbs and along the local stretch of the Great Indian Peninsular Railway, and showed police exactly where he had committed them.

A police surgeon assessed Raghav as sane and able to understand the nature and purpose of his actions. A psychiatrist acting for the defence disagreed, asserting that Raghav was a long-term sufferer of schizophrenia and afflicted by delusions to the extent that he couldn't understand that his actions were morally or legally wrong. The court tried to settle the matter by referring Raghav to a panel of three psychiatrists, who reported that he was in thrall to a series of delusions characterized by notions of persecution and self-importance. Inter alia, Raghav believed that various governments were persecuting him with temptations and had brought him to Mumbai to commit crime, that he was in himself a cosmic power, or "Shakti", that homosexual relations would turn him into a woman, and that he was a citizen of "Kanoon", a distinctly different world to the one in which his questioners lived.

There seems little doubt that Raman Raghav was a visionary serial killer. Elements such as planning, ideology, prolonged sadism, material gain and cunning that typify other categories of serial killing were absent from Raghav's crimes. His murders could conceivably have been mission-oriented but Raghav's victims were his own people – those who were experiencing desperation, poverty and itinerancy – and not a distinctly different type of people to whom blame for his misfortunes might be attached. While the impact of his delusions on his capacity to form criminal intent might be debated, the chaotic and seemingly purposeless nature of his killings is distinctly visionary.

The Indian judicial system grappled with questions like these over decades. Raghav was initially sentenced to death but this was commuted to life imprisonment in 1987 due to his declining mental health. He died of kidney failure in 1995 having shed no further light on his actions or the fates of an unknown number of unnamed and un-mourned victims.

It is perhaps appropriate that whatever force impelled Raghav to visit lethal violence on so many poor souls – against whom he had no clear animus – will remain forever opaque. It is in the nature of visionary killers that they operate in a thick grey fog of delusion, dislocation and dissociation. This, perhaps, is the reason why visionary killings are so chilling. We seek the solace of reason, of cause and effect, and the idea that the blameless can be killed without any rationale that we can understand can and should make us uneasy.

CHAPTER TWO:

MISSION-ORIENTED SERIAL KILLERS

THE MIND OF A MISSION-ORIENTED KILLER

In Greek mythology, Sisyphus, an ancient king of Corinth, angered the gods by violently abusing guests and thereby violating his sacred duty of hospitality. They punished him by granting him eternal life with a catch: he would have to spend his days pushing an immense rock up a hill only to see it roll back down again, and to repeat this soul-destroying, pointless grind forever. The term "Sisyphean" can therefore be applied to any task that seems both arduous and futile.

The French philosopher Albert Camus had a different take on the ordeal of Sisyphus. Writing in 1942 and influenced by the upheavals and horrors of the Second World War, Camus contrasted the innate human need to find meaning with the universe's utter indifference to this need. He suggested that Sisyphus should be considered happy and fulfilled for he has an all-consuming purpose. Given the wildly improbable odds against the typical human finding a purpose that makes an iota of difference to the world, most of us should be content if we have a purpose that consumes us, no matter how trivial or absurd it is.

Mission-oriented killers in their own perverse ways could be said to have taken this philosophical lesson to heart. Unlike visionary killers, they are not impelled by delusion and governed by chaos; they are almost precisely the opposite, for they have a specific purpose and apply it in a calculating, systematic and careful manner. This is not to say that mission-oriented killers don't have their own hinterland of abuse and pathology, but their murderous impulses are focused by careful planning and a commitment to their cause bordering on ideological. What typifies mission-oriented killers is the notion that the world needs to be cleansed of a particular type of victim. They carefully stalk and quickly kill their victims and are less inclined towards the sustained torture and abuse that typify power-oriented and hedonistic killers. Where there is pre-mortem violence, it is born of spontaneous rage rather than planned sadism.

Mikhail Popkov, the prolific Siberian serial killer, may have been raised by an abusive mother with alcoholism and developed a murderous animus against drunken women that would inspire him to systematically exploit his power and status as a police officer to murder 83 women and children over a twenty-year period. Peter Sutcliffe, the so-called Yorkshire Ripper, learned from and exceeded his father's tendencies towards misogynistic coercion, violence and debasement, and treated his mother's indulgence with contempt. Sutcliffe expressed his loathing by targeting women walking alone, usually but not always after dark – and sometimes but not always earning from sex work – and took enough care to evade the UK's largest ever manhunt for five years despite being interviewed nine times.

In New York and the US Midwest in the nineteenth century, Belle Gunness's single-minded devotion to stealing money, first by insurance fraud and later by false offers of marriage, made her a moderately wealthy serial murderer of 14 men and children. In the late 1970s, Joseph Paul Franklin killed a suspected total of 22 victims across a number of US states, targeting Black and Jewish people and inspired by the notion that racial mixing was an offence against God.

INSIDE THE MINDS OF SERIAL KILLERS

Read on to delve into the minds of killers whose murders are distinguished by a particularly vivid form of evil: unswerving and cold-eyed self-righteousness. These killers made a vocation of killing and got to enjoy the contentment that comes from all-consuming purpose. There is nothing in human nature or Camus' philosophical model that stops that purpose being murderous.

MIKHAIL POPKOV: THE ANGARSK MANIAC

Between 1992 and 2012, Mikhail Viktorovich Popkov sexually assaulted and murdered at least 83 women and girls in the vast Russian region of Siberia. He killed over a long period of time and across various cities and areas including Vladivostok, Irkutsk and Angarsk; he is referred to by the Russian media as the Angarsk Maniac. He remains the most prolific individual serial killer in the history of Russia and the USSR.

Mikhail Popkov was born in 1964 in the Krasnoyarsk Krai region of Siberia in what was then the USSR. His formative years are shrouded in mystery, but it has been speculated that he was abused by a mother who had alcoholism, as he developed a murderous animus against visibly drunken women that he would enact time and time again as an adult. He was an archetypal mission-oriented serial killer, devoting himself to torturing and exterminating a specific category of his fellow citizens, in his case women under the influence of alcohol. He explicitly claimed to be following his convictions by purging the streets of immoral women.

While Popkov's obsession is irrational and morally repugnant, he was methodical, disciplined, persistent and able to plausibly lead a double life and escape detection for decades. Far from being at the mercy of delusion and chaos, he both held down a job as a police officer and made that job a key aspect of his modus operandi. So determined a misogynist was Popkov that he stretched his own definition of female immorality; women socializing without male chaperones would meet his criteria, particularly if their body types were similar to his mother's.

Most of Popkov's murders occurred in Angarsk, where he was employed as a police officer. He would go out after dark in his police uniform, sometimes using a police vehicle, and offer lifts to victims who fitted his profile. They were driven to remote areas, where they would be degraded, tortured and killed with implements ranging from screwdrivers and baseball bats to hunting knives, awls, slipknots and hatchets before being violated post-mortem. Popkov's hatred for his victims manifested itself in degrees of mutilation that earned him the nickname Werewolf. He was also known as the Wednesday Murderer, as many of his victims were found on this day of the week.

Popkov's role as a police officer not only facilitated his murders but helped him stay a step or two ahead of the murder investigation and, on occasion, disrupt it. He was free to enact his bloody obsession for two decades, despite a large-scale police inquiry and useful testimony from a few survivors who survived or at least lived long enough to testify before succumbing to their injuries. Eventually, the fact that track marks from a standard police vehicle were found at many crime scenes obliged investigators to confront an ugly truth head-on. In 2012, 3,500 serving and former police officers were obliged to give DNA samples; Popkov, by then a security guard, was matched to crime-scene semen samples and arrested.

Siberian police were roundly criticized for failing to give credence to clear evidence that the Angarsk Maniac was one of their own. It would not be the first nor the last time that an unwillingness to think the unthinkable would cost lives. It is a striking feature of mission-oriented serial killers that, far from being outwardly if quietly normal, they can be well-regarded, outgoing and charming members of their community.

Mikhail Popkov was married to Elena Popkova, with whom he had a daughter, Ekaterina. One of his victims, known as Svetlana M, was stripped and mauled by Popkov, who then dashed her head against a tree and left her for dead in the Siberian winter; miraculously, she was found and eventually regained consciousness in a medical facility. Popkov was clearly being considered as a suspect by investigators, because they showed his photograph to Svetlana M and she identified him as her assailant. Unfortunately, however, Elena Popkova was not just a devoted wife but also a police officer herself. How much Elena understood of her husband's true nature can only be speculated upon, and the possibility that she herself was coerced cannot be ruled out; when she gave Popkov an alibi for the near murder of Svetlana M, however, justice was denied a little longer and more young women were doomed. Both Elena and Ekaterina have since appeared on Russian television to insist they harboured no suspicions about Popkov.

In 2015, Popkov was convicted of 22 murders and sentenced to life imprisonment. In captivity, he confessed to another 59 murders and was convicted of 56 of them. In a grisly coda, Popkov has claimed that his killings stopped long before he was arrested, as he contracted syphilis during an act of necrophilia; this sapped his lust and with it his desire to kill.

Even behind bars, Popkov still has chutzpah; the BBC and others reported in 2018 that he aimed to appeal his latest sentence with the aim of retaining his 24,000 roubles per month police pension. He has also enjoyed his day trips from prison, touring the countryside and pointing out copses, swamps and lakes from which bodies might be recovered.

It is traditional in Russia for coffins to remain open until they are laid in the ground so that mourners can see the loved one to whom they are saying a final farewell. For the majority of Popkov's victims, closed coffins were insisted upon lest mourners be horrified by what the Angarsk Maniac had wrought.

The origins of Popkov's mission remain somewhat opaque, even though the underlying misogyny is searingly clear. According to the now defunct *Siberian Times*, detectives accepted that his killings were his way of taking vicarious revenge against his abusive mother, who had alcoholism. Quoted in *HuffPost* in 2017, Angarsk psychiatrist Alexander Grishin speculated that "maybe in his childhood other drunk women abused him too, and all this affected his behaviour later in his adult life and led to such horrible consequences".

Whatever the underlying pathology, however, the most haunting aspect of mission-oriented serial killers like Popkov may be this: those who know them as neighbours, workmates or friends are often profoundly shocked to discover their true nature. To put it another way: the existence of killers as amiable and matter-of-fact as Popkov means that your fishing friend, your fellow dog walker, your gym buddy or any other normal, relatable figure from your day-to-day life could have a diabolical mission of their own.

BELLE GUNNESS: NORDIC NOIR

"*Vikingr*" is an Old Norse word meaning "freebooter" or "coastal raider". For those who sailed with swords and spears from the hard, hungry lands of latter-day Scandinavia in the early medieval period, "Viking" was a verb and to "go Viking" meant to strike out for richer lands and hack your fortune out of the rich earth or the rich locals. There was of course more to the Viking age than this; indeed, the settled Norse kingdoms of late medieval Europe sometimes called themselves "*Ostmen*" while using "Viking" pejoratively to mean "pirate".

Belle Gunness lived and died long after the age of the Vikings, but she might just have channelled the instincts of some of her more ruthless ancestors. This Norwegian-American serial killer dispatched at least 14 victims in Illinois and Indiana, USA, between 1884 and 1908. It has been speculated that she may have killed up to 40 people and contrived to escape justice by faking her own death. Much is uncertain about her story, but one fact is clear: she is one of history's most prolific, ruthless and calculating female serial killers.

Belle Gunness was born Brynhild Paulsdatter Størseth in 1859 in Selbu, Norway, between that country's North Atlantic coast and Jämtland in Sweden. As a teenager, Brynhild decided she would seek her fortune in New York City and worked hard for years on cattle farms until she could afford to take ship. In 1881, while in her early twenties, she finally arrived at Castle Garden, Manhattan, USA, the immigration depot that preceded the famous Ellis Island. She changed her first name to Belle for simplicity's sake and found work as a domestic servant while staying with relatives in Chicago.

Domestic servitude was never to Belle's taste and she soon moved on to dismembering carcasses for a butcher. Here, she practised tradecraft that would serve her well as a serial killer, and she was physically well equipped for it. Belle stood at 1.7 m (5 ft 7 in.), a respectable height for a nineteenth-century woman, and her life of hard manual work had made her stocky and strong. Long days spent skinning, eviscerating and splitting animals hung from hooks with the stench of blood and effluent in her nostrils didn't faze Belle.

While Belle Gunness is regarded as a mission-oriented serial killer, she bore no particular grudge against one type of person over another. She was instead fixated on enriching herself and hit upon murder as a reliable way of achieving it. In 1884, Belle married Mads Sørensen and together they acquired a home and a candy store, both of which mysteriously burned down, netting the couple significant insurance payouts. Larcenous conduct took on a lethal aspect soon thereafter: two of Belle's babies died suddenly, their symptoms consistent with poisoning, and she was financially rewarded, having insured both their lives.

The prospect of a mother killing her babies for an insurance payout must have seemed wildly improbable to the authorities and, in any case, infant mortality was far more prevalent and forensic science far less developed than today. As if the notion of Belle killing her own flesh and blood wasn't disturbing enough, neighbourhood gossips insisted it was far worse than that – she had never appeared pregnant and the babies might not have been hers.

The extent of Sørensen's complicity in Belle's murderous insurance racket can't be ascertained, as he didn't live to offer any insight. One summer's day in 1900, Sørensen complained of a headache and was given a medicinal powder by Belle, after which he died of a cerebral haemorrhage. It just so happened that Sørensen died in the brief period of overlap between one life insurance policy expiring and another beginning. Belle collected on both policies, netting a total of US$5,000 (approximately US$185,000 in 2024) with which she bought a pig farm in La Porte, Indiana.

Belle's killing began to resemble a dark farce. She married Peter Gunness in April 1902 and within the week his infant daughter died of unascertainable causes in his new wife's care. Peter followed his daughter later that year when, it was claimed, a meat grinder fell from a shelf and shattered his skull. It is not known whether Belle was indifferent to suspicion about her brazen killings or just contemptuous of the power of law enforcement to stop her. In either case, while a local coroner suspected murder, nothing could be proved and Belle collected a handsome insurance payout of US$3,000 (approximately US$110,000 in 2024).

In 1905, Belle upped the ante. She placed advertisements in Chicago newspapers inviting eligible gentlemen to correspond with her with a view to visiting her farm and proposing marriage. It is unfortunate that the small print of an Edwardian newspaper's back pages could not convey local history and gossip. First to respond was a Wisconsin farmhand named Henry Gurholt, who set off for La Porte in good health and high hopes and wasn't seen again. When the Gurholt family made enquiries with Belle, she told them that he'd visited her, then headed off to Chicago, having inexplicably left behind his valuables. A year later, John Moe of Minnesota made a similar journey, having been persuaded to bring all the cash he could raise. Moe was never seen again, although he too had left his valuables with Belle, presumably for safekeeping.

In the spring of 1908, fire tore through Belle's La Porte farmhouse and the charred remains of a headless woman and three children were found inside. Within days, newspaper reports that had sought to beatify Belle Gunness as an exemplary mother who had died trying to save her young had to be urgently reassessed. At least 11 more sets of human remains were found buried around the farm, most unidentifiable. Each body had been butchered in a proficient and consistent manner, as if by someone with relevant experience.

La Porte law enforcement found the 11 bodies only because of the brave and persistent Asle Helgelien. Her brother, Andrew, had gone missing and she'd found correspondence from Belle urging him to secretly join her with whatever money he could bring. Initially, Asle had searched the Gunness farm with the help of an equally suspicious former farmhand. She had dug into a suspicious depression in a pig pen, uncovered a sack, emptied it and been confronted by her brother's severed head along with his hands and feet.

Law enforcement was compelled to act. In the absence of Belle Gunness, they detained Belle's farmhand and sometime lover, Ray Lamphere, and charged him with the murder of

Belle and her children. He confessed that Belle's marriage advertisements had been a means of bringing men to her doorstep so that she could rob and murder them. Belle, he alleged, had been told that a relative of one of her victims was investigating her; she had panicked and asked Lamphere to burn down the farmhouse so that she could pretend to be dead and disappear.

While La Porte's sheriff dismissed the notion that Belle Gunness had faked her death and escaped, the doctor performing the post-mortem maintained that the body he examined was significantly shorter and lighter than the tall and stocky Belle. When arrested, Ray Lamphere had been wearing Moe's coat and Gurholt's watch. He may therefore be considered lucky that he was convicted only of arson, but that luck was fickle as he died of tuberculosis (TB) in the Michigan City Penitentiary 20 months after Belle's disappearance.

The old Latin phrase "*radix malorum est cupiditas*" translates as "the love of money is the root of all evil". Belle Gunness personified this idea, almost certainly killing her husband, possibly killing her own or someone else's babies and definitely killing a remarkable number of strangers, all in her single-minded pursuit of an unspectacular degree of wealth.

There remains the slight but nonetheless galling possibility that this money-minded killer got to enjoy a comfortable and financially secure old age. If she did indeed fool the authorities once again and flee, she might have approved of the fact that the human charnel house she'd created became a tourist attraction, haunted by money-grubbing hucksters and sellers of tawdry souvenirs, all cashing in on death.

DANIEL GONZALEZ: THE FREDDY KRUEGER KILLER

Between 15 and 17 September 2004, Daniel Gonzalez stabbed four strangers to death in separate incidents in London and Sussex, England. It was alleged that he had sought fame by emulating the fictional supernatural killer Freddy Krueger from the *Nightmare on Elm Street* film series.

Gonzalez is generally regarded as a mission-oriented serial killer. Killers in this category have a mission that has long-term, logical consistency despite being irrational and immoral. That mission is often founded in formative trauma, disassociation or grievance and might single out specific categories of people ranging from sex workers to the homeless. Gonzalez's mission is less clear-cut; beyond a superficial desire to emulate a celluloid slasher and make himself a household name, his aims lacked coherence. All that his victims had in common was that they were mostly elderly and incapable of resistance.

Daniel Gonzalez was born in Woking, Surrey, England, in 1980 to an English mother and Spanish father. He did well at school, becoming a confident stage actor and a chess champion, but by his mid-teenage years his mental state had become a matter of concern. Dark moods and disturbing thoughts led to clinical intervention, despite which he dropped out of society and adopted an unhealthy lifestyle.

By the age of 24, Gonzalez was unemployed and unemployable and filled the empty hours by taking drugs, playing video games and watching slasher films. On 15 September 2004, 61-year-old Peter King was walking his dog in Hillsea, Hampshire, when Gonzalez approached and announced his intention to kill him. Peter fought off his assailant and fortunately survived, but he had experienced the beginning of Gonzalez's itinerant stabbing campaign. Later the same day, Gonzalez surfaced in Hove, East Sussex, where he donned a hockey mask in a bid to look like another fictional slasher, Jason Voorhees from the *Friday the 13th* film series. So equipped, he stabbed to death 76-year-old Marie Harding and returned to his home in Woking.

On 17 September 2004, Gonzalez travelled to London and went on a rampage. At 5.30 a.m., he approached 46-year-old Kevin Molloy in Tottenham and stabbed him repeatedly in the head, neck and chest, leaving him to bleed to death in the street. At 7 a.m., Koumis Constantino was confronted by a knife-wielding home invader, fought back and was lucky to survive with only an arm injury. By 8 a.m., Gonzalez had made his way to Highgate, where, after trying and failing to access other houses, he found his way into the home of retired couple Derek and Jean Robinson and stabbed them both to death.

Gonzalez was very far from the stereotypical image of a methodical, forensically aware serial killer. He ran naked and bloody from the Robinsons' home in Highgate and was arrested soon after at the Tottenham Court Road tube station. Even in custody, Gonzalez's appetite for bloody violence did not abate. While awaiting trial he was held at Broadmoor Hospital, a high-security psychiatric facility that has housed some of the world's most infamous killers. Here, he attempted suicide by biting through his radial artery and could be handled only by prison officers in body armour.

An argument could be made for classing Gonzalez as a visionary rather than a mission-oriented serial killer, and indeed his defence team tried and failed to make the case that he was guilty not of murder but of manslaughter by reason of diminished responsibility. Murder trials often bring this tangled issue into sharp focus; there is a disconnect between how insanity is treated by the medical and legal professions.

At the Gonzalez trial, the prosecution made the case that Gonzalez was a psychopath who had disinhibited himself with alcohol and drugs but had nevertheless formed the requisite intent for murder. They also asserted that Gonzalez had tried to vitiate his responsibility by pretending to court-appointed psychiatrists that he'd been commanded by voices in his head. It was found that Gonzalez had sufficient capacity for a murder conviction and he was given six life sentences with a judicial recommendation that he should never be released.

By the letter of the law in many countries, if a defendant is capable of controlling their actions and understanding the difference between right and wrong then, regardless of the effects of drink, drugs and severe mental illness, they are criminally responsible. It could be argued that, if the effect of mental illness on criminal intent is being debated at a murder trial, then it's already too late and something fundamental has gone wrong in how that society polices and cares for its citizens.

In the aftermath, Gonzalez's mother, Lesley Savage, was quoted by the BBC and other news media. "Every time we asked for help for Daniel," she said, "we were told we would have to wait for a crisis to occur." She had taken various desperate measures to try to get Gonzalez the psychiatric care he plainly needed, including a plea to social services featuring a prophetic question: "Does my son have to commit murder to get help?"

On 9 August 2007, Gonzalez finally succeeded in taking his own life, opening an artery with the snapped edge of a CD case and expiring in a pool of his own blood.

PETER SUTCLIFFE: THE YORKSHIRE RIPPER

Between 1975 and 1980, Peter Sutcliffe murdered 13 women and attempted to murder seven others in West Yorkshire and Greater Manchester in the UK. He is best known by the moniker the Yorkshire Ripper, bestowed on him by the British tabloid press in reference to the unidentified serial killer known as Jack the Ripper who haunted Whitechapel, London, in the 1880s.

Peter Sutcliffe was born in Shipley, West Yorkshire, in 1946. Both his parents were religiously observant but differed in their worship: John Sutcliffe was Anglican and Kathleen Coonan was Catholic. John was also a violent, sanctimonious, bullying womanizer and binge drinker who routinely assaulted his partner and children. Kathleen, by contrast, cossetted Peter, inviting taunts from John that he was an unmanly mummy's boy. Peter's relationship with his parents remained off-kilter even in adult life. In 1970, 24-year-old Peter was invited to a honeytrap set by his father for his mother: John had posed as Kathleen's secret lover and invited her to an assignation at a hotel, where he confronted her with her lingerie and two of her grown-up children.

Sutcliffe was a clear-cut, mission-oriented serial killer. While he would be diagnosed with schizophrenia prior to his murder trial, neither the judge nor the jury would accept that his killings had been driven by delusion sufficient in degree to vitiate criminal intent. His dysfunctional upbringing set him on a path to emulating and exceeding his father's tendencies towards coercion, violence and debasement. Peter Sutcliffe was a committed misogynist fascinated by sex work. He cut his teeth on voyeurism, spending his idle hours as a young man spying on sex workers with their clients, then later escalated to murdering sex workers in a systematic and organized manner. It is of note that he tended not to procure sexual services from sex workers; he derived gratification from either watching or killing them.

Sutcliffe cut an isolated, awkward figure at school and left at the age of 15 to embark on a series of basic jobs, including a spell as a gravedigger in the 1960s. For those who handle the dead, a judicious degree of graveyard humour is de rigueur; Sutcliffe, however, pushed the boundaries, appalling his colleagues with his overfamiliarity with the dead and his enthusiasm for long overtime hours spent cleansing cadavers. He went on to work in factories before retraining as a truck driver in the mid-1970s.

In 1974, Sutcliffe married his long-term girlfriend, Sonia Szurma. It seems that, while he was busy roaming Northern England as a secret, murderous misogynist, at home he may have been on the receiving end of domestic violence. Sonia's plans to become a teacher were delayed by a diagnosis of schizophrenia, and, while it is not known precisely how she managed the condition, it is known that she was prone to unpredictable rages and would assault Peter both privately and publicly.

Sutcliffe's first attack on a sex worker was well documented and also brought about the first of many frustratingly fruitless interactions with police officers. In 1969, he assaulted a sex worker in Bradford, West Yorkshire, while purporting to look for someone who'd stolen cash from him. The friend's vehicle in which Sutcliffe had fled the scene was identified and he was tracked down by police, who gave him a dressing down and told him he was lucky as charges weren't being pressed.

In July 1975, a year into married life and a few months after being made redundant from a factory job, Sutcliffe escalated his offending and settled on a modus operandi. After dark on 5 July 1975, he stalked Anna Rogulskyj, 36, as she walked alone in Keighley, West Yorkshire. He struck her head with a hammer, almost killing her, then slashed her stomach with a blade. Sutcliffe was disturbed by a concerned neighbour and fled, and Anna's life was saved by emergency brain surgery.

On the night of 15 August 1975 in Halifax, Sutcliffe stalked Olive Smelt, 46, distracted her with small talk, then smashed her skull with a hammer and slashed at her lower back. He was once again interrupted and took to his heels, leaving his grievously injured and traumatized victim alive. It is of note that, while neither of these women was a sex worker and neither was walking in a red-light area, and even though Olive told police that her assailant had a Yorkshire accent, these facts would be ignored for far too long.

Tracy Browne, 14, had a fateful encounter with Sutcliffe in Silsden near Bradford on 27 August 1975. He sidled up alongside her as she walked along a remote country road, and they enjoyed a relaxed conversation during which time she became familiar with his accent, manner, cast of features, height, build and clothing. He then produced a hammer and landed multiple blows on the back of her skull. Once again, he was spooked by unexpected passers-by and fled, and his victim survived thanks to emergency brain surgery. Once again, the police would disregard Tracy's evidence as it didn't fit the preferred narrative, and Sutcliffe wasn't convicted of this assault until he confessed to it in 1992.

Sutcliffe committed his first known murder on 30 October 1975. Wilma McCann, 28, was walking past playing fields in the Chapeltown area of Leeds after dark when Sutcliffe landed lethal hammer blows on the base of her skull. On 20 January 1976 in Leeds, Sutcliffe committed his second murder and his first known murder of a sex worker. Emily Jackson, 42, had been induced by her husband into selling her body on the city's streets to bolster family finances. Sutcliffe picked her up in his vehicle at Roundhay Park, Leeds, drove her to a semi-derelict industrial estate and killed her in a scorching burst of rage. He broke her skull with a hammer, stabbed her repeatedly with a screwdriver and finally stamped on her so hard that he left a good impression of the sole of a boot.

On 9 May 1976, Sutcliffe persuaded another victim into his car in Roundhay Park. Marcella Claxton, 20, was beaten with a hammer and, while she was lucky to survive, she miscarried a baby. Sutcliffe's modus operandi and a pattern of nocturnal horror were now established. Decades later, those who lived through those times and in that region of the UK still vividly remember the taint of terror attached to urban streets after dark. For young women in particular, the sense that walking unaccompanied after dark could expose them to a remorseless killer from whom the police could seemingly offer no protection was pervasive and long-lasting. After dark on 12 November 1977 in 11 towns across the UK, women critical of perceived victim-blaming by the police held Reclaim the Night marches.

Despite what would become the prevailing narrative, Sutcliffe did not prey exclusively on sex workers. West Yorkshire Police were criticized at the time and subsequently both for confirmation bias as to the nature and extent of Sutcliffe's offending and for seeing murdered sex workers as second-class citizens worthy of less concern. Taken together with the warping effect of media involvement on the minds and priorities of senior detectives, these failings would lead the police to exclude good evidence that could have led to an earlier resolution and saved lives.

On 5 February 1977, Sutcliffe murdered 28-year-old sex worker Irene Richardson in Roundhay Park and left tyre tracks near the scene. On 23 April 1977, in a minor departure from his modus operandi, he murdered 32-year-old sex worker Patricia Atkinson-Mitra in her Bradford apartment and left a boot print on her bedding. On 25 June 1977 in Leeds, 16-year-old Jayne MacDonald missed the last bus home and disappeared after deciding to walk home. Her body was later found in a Chapeltown playground; in addition to his usual pattern of violence, Sutcliffe had forced a broken bottle into her chest.

The grim litany of tabloid stories grew longer and opportunities kept being missed. On 10 July 1977, Sutcliffe struck 43-year-old Maureen Long with a hammer but was disturbed and left her for dead. She survived and a witness's faulty recollection led 300 police officers to check thousands of cars of the wrong make. On 1 October 1977, Sutcliffe crossed the Pennine Hills and murdered sex worker Jean Jordan, 20, in the Chorlton-cum-Hardy area of Greater Manchester. He later realized he'd left a traceable banknote on Jean's body and, despite taking the risk of returning to the scene, was unable to find it.

That banknote led to a significant narrowing of the suspect pool. Jean Jordan had secreted it in a hidden compartment of her handbag. In a pre-digital time, many employees were paid in cash and that cash was issued by banks to specific companies in a traceable manner. Of the workers who could have received the banknote in their pay packets, 5,000 were men. Each one of them was interviewed by police officers, including Sutcliffe, who gave a sufficiently convincing alibi. Once again, the spotlight alighted momentarily on him then moved away.

On 14 December 1977, Sutcliffe tried to murder 25-year-old sex worker Marilyn Moore in Leeds but slipped while trying to deliver a final blow, allowing her to escape and survive despite severe injuries. Not only did he once again leave distinctive tyre tracks at the scene, but Marilyn gave a strong description of both Sutcliffe and his car, a Sunbeam Rapier. Although Sutcliffe kept getting lucky breaks, it seems with hindsight that the net was closing and his arrest had to be imminent. This, alas, was not the case and more breaks would come his way.

Sutcliffe persisted, undeterred. On 21 January 1978 in Bradford, he killed 21-year-old sex worker Yvonne Ann Pearson by beating her with a hammer and forcing horsehair – commonly used to stuff furniture – into her mouth. On 31 January 1978 in Huddersfield, West Yorkshire, he deviated again from his modus operandi. He landed hammer blows on the head of 18-year-old sex worker Helen Rytka, violated her, beat her again, then stabbed her in the heart and lungs. Helen was the only victim raped by Sutcliffe. On 16 May 1978 in a hospital car park in Chorlton-on-Medlock, Greater Manchester, Sutcliffe beat and stabbed 40-year-old sex worker Vera Evelyn Millward to death.

On 2 March 1979, 22-year-old student Ann Rooney was attacked by Sutcliffe in Horsforth, Leeds. She survived and provided yet another excellent description of Sutcliffe and his Sunbeam Rapier. Not only had Sutcliffe been interviewed several times, but his car had been repeatedly noted in trawls of red-light areas of West Yorkshire. While the investigation ground laboriously through its gears, Sutcliffe killed again. On 4 April 1979 in Halifax, 19-year-old office worker Josephine Whitaker was beaten and stabbed to death in what might have been Sutcliffe's most savage attack; her skull was split from ear to ear and she had been stabbed in the most intimate way imaginable.

The Yorkshire Ripper's reign of terror might have ended in 1979 but for an eccentric intervention and a flailing police response. A hoaxer sent a recorded message to West Yorkshire Police's assistant chief constable, George Oldfield, purporting to be "Jack" and taunting him for his failure to catch him. The same hoaxer sent a series of equally unhelpful letters to both the police and the *Daily Mirror* newspaper. Linguistic experts narrowed the hoaxer's accent down to a specific area of North East England and he was thus christened Wearside Jack. In 2005, Wearside Jack would be identified by DNA analysis as John Humble of Sunderland, an unemployed person with alcoholism. He was found guilty of attempting to pervert the course of justice and jailed. He was emphatically not guilty of any of Sutcliffe's crimes, but he did succeed in diverting enormous police resources towards a vast and wholly erroneous new body of potential suspects.

On went the killings. On 1 September 1979 in Bradford, Sutcliffe claimed his eleventh victim, 20-year-old student Barbara Leach. He battered her around the head with a hammer, dragged her into a backyard, sexually degraded her, then stabbed her to death with a screwdriver. On 26 June 1980, Sutcliffe was arrested for drink-driving but still remained at large pending trial. On 20 August 1980 near Farsley, Leeds, Sutcliffe murdered 47-year-old civil servant Marguerite Walls. He beat her with a hammer while repeatedly yelling "filthy prostitute", then suffocated and stripped her. On 24 September 1980 in Headingley, Leeds, he tried and failed to murder 34-year-old doctor Upadhya Bandara in a similar manner.

By the autumn of 1980, Sutcliffe's campaign of horror was nearing its end. On 25 October 1980 in Leeds, 21-year-old student Maureen Lea woke up in hospital with a punctured skull, a broken jaw and numerous other injuries, having been attacked in Chapeltown. On 5 November 1980, 16-year-old Theresa Sykes had her skull broken in Oakes, Huddersfield, but was saved when her boyfriend heard her screams. On 17 November 1980 in Headingley, Leeds, Sutcliffe may have claimed his last victim when he killed 20-year-old student Jacqueline Hill. In yet another horrific variation, her many wounds included being stabbed in the eye with the same screwdriver Sutcliffe had used on other victims.

Before his final arrest, Sutcliffe was interviewed nine times as part of the Ripper inquiry and ruled out as a suspect. On 2 January 1981, he was stopped in his car by police in a red-light area of Sheffield, South Yorkshire, in the company of sex worker Olivia Reivers. While the officers examined his car, Sutcliffe was allowed to step behind an oil tank, having claimed he needed to urinate. His car was found to be on false plates and he was arrested, transferred to West Yorkshire and interviewed for the tenth time as part of the Ripper inquiry. While Sutcliffe was still in custody, an officer followed a hunch, went to the scene of the arrest and discovered a kill kit comprising a hammer, a knife and a rope at the spot where Sutcliffe had supposedly gone to relieve himself. He was also discovered to have secreted a knife behind a cistern at Dewsbury Police Station while answering yet another call of nature.

Sutcliffe was questioned at length and in detail and ultimately confessed to the 13 murders and seven attempted murders with which he would be charged, furnishing abundant detail and claiming that God had commanded him to cleanse the streets of sex workers. His defence team asserted that he was guilty not of murder but of manslaughter on the grounds of diminished responsibility, relying on multiple diagnoses of schizophrenia. Despite this, the presiding judge rejected the psychiatric advice and slated the case for trial by jury. The jury also rejected the clinical diagnoses and found Sutcliffe guilty as charged. He was sentenced to life imprisonment and died in 2020 at the age of 74.

The 1982 Byford Report into the Ripper investigation made many recommendations that have improved the conduct of complex police investigations and probably saved many lives. It acknowledged that those working in a paper-based, overworked and data-saturated incident room were not capable of making sense of useful information in a timely manner, an issue that subsequent police IT systems were designed specifically to remedy. It made the point that appointing an investigative lead based on seniority and age rather than specialization and competence was unhelpful. George Oldfield was singled out for his dogmatic focus on Wearside Jack to the exclusion of messier, more complex and ultimately more profitable lines of enquiry. In persisting with this canard, Oldfield ignored survivor testimony and expert advice.

The hunt for Sutcliffe mushroomed into one of the largest and costliest murder inquiries in UK history. It is important to emphasize that crime fiction bears little relation to the reality of police homicide inquiries. Murders aren't solved by celebrity detectives ambushing well-heeled suspects in genteel drawing rooms with quivers full of piercing insights. Nor are they solved by maverick geniuses stumbling and mumbling their way through personal crises until flashes of otherworldly genius illuminate everything in a dramatically tidy manner.

Effective murder inquiries are open-minded, open-ended trawls through a vast sea of data. They consume decades of working time, a beef herd's worth of shoe leather, lakes of ink and, even in the digital age, mountains of paper. There is always space for instinct and insight, but only within a structure designed to ensure that nothing is missed in the headlong pursuit of a simple, urgent prosecution. As Pablo Picasso put it, "inspiration exists, but it has to find you working."

It is of note that in a modern murder inquiry in the UK, at least one officer will be in charge of analyzing and indexing unused material, items that will not be used as prosecution evidence but will still need to be disclosed to the defence. Practices like these alert the defence to items that might help their case but be inconvenient to, or even contradict, the prosecution. They also help to ward off the spectre of confirmation bias.

It is in the nature of humanity and its institutions to seek out evidence that supports desirable or expedient beliefs and to jettison or simply fail to see anything that contradicts such beliefs. The culture and mores of the UK and its police forces in the 1970s, together with technology and procedures that were not sufficiently insulated from confirmation bias, are the backdrop to the story of the so-called Yorkshire Ripper. These issues undoubtedly delayed his being brought to justice and thereby sealed the fate of multiple murder victims.

There is another unsavoury strand to this story, however. For the mass media, murder has always been a commercial boon, and serial killings especially so. Crime coverage in news outlets, no matter the demographic or political persuasion of the readership, almost always goes far beyond necessary public information in its scope. It might be argued that it also creates and indulges a voyeuristic and prurient demand for horrific and intimate detail. All of these issues played their part in the harrowing tale of the Yorkshire Ripper.

The distinct possibility remains that Sutcliffe's tally of death and suffering may never be fully appreciated. Subsequent internal police reviews, beginning with a confidential investigation by senior detective Keith Hellawell in 1982, estimated that Sutcliffe may have committed up to 22 unsolved murders and attempted murders.

When the death, suffering, horror, culture shock and long-term legacy for British law enforcement and society are considered in retrospect, Peter Sutcliffe's 13 confirmed murders had a seismic impact. At the heart of the matter, however, remains a simple question: why? Could a seemingly ordinary, outwardly respectable man be impelled to plumb such depths of depravity by his father's abusive contempt for his mother, by the early normalization of voyeurism, by a fascination with sex work and ultimately by a loathing for his own warped needs, projected savagely onto others? The answer, chillingly, appears to be yes.

GARY RIDGWAY: THE GREEN RIVER KILLER

Gary Ridgway is known to have murdered 49 women and children in a sustained and determined career of killing in the USA's Pacific Northwest between 1982 and 2001 and may have murdered many more. Due to the fact that several of his victims were found in Washington State's Green River, he is popularly known as the Green River Killer.

The majority of Ridgway's victims were young or underage females who were either sex workers or desperate, isolated and vulnerable. Ridgway was morbidly preoccupied with – and resentful of – sex workers, actively despising them while frequently using their services. He was also a paraphiliac, known to have returned to the remains of his victims to indulge in necrophilia.

Gary Ridgway was born in 1949 in Salt Lake City, Utah, and endured an unsettled childhood. His mother was aggressively domineering and the relationship between his parents was fiery. They also instilled in young Gary a conflict between lust and shame that would never be resolved. While his father's complaints about sex workers on the streets were persistent enough to suggest a prurient fascination, his mother taught him acute sexual shame. Ridgway wetted the bed until well into puberty, and his mother would wash his genitals with forceful contempt. He would later claim that, from an early age, he had harboured both lust and murderous anger for his mother. It may also be significant that Ridgway's upbringing was religiously observant; Christian notions of sexual probity and the idea that God was watching might well have given his gnawing sense of shame more bite.

Psychiatrist J. M. Macdonald suggested in 1963 that bed-wetting in late childhood is one of three predictors of serial violence. While Ridgway is not believed to have exhibited the other two predictors – zoosadism and fire-starting – he did demonstrate an early preoccupation with violence. At the age of 16, he led a six-year-old child into woodland and stabbed him in the liver, telling the victim with a grin that he had always wanted to know what it felt like to kill. The victim survived and there appear to have been no criminal sanctions for Ridgway. However, this underachieving boy of low intelligence, schooled in shame by his mother's rough hands, had learned how he might achieve power and pleasure.

Despite having to repeat a year at high school, Ridgway did manage to graduate in 1969 and married his girlfriend, Claudia Barrows, in 1970. He also enlisted in the US Navy and saw combat during the Vietnam War. As a young adult, he developed a seemingly insatiable taste for risky intercourse with sex workers. He repeatedly contracted gonorrhoea, suggesting that he found bareback, or unprotected, sex with risky partners a particular thrill. Perhaps being in thrall to his lust with shameful, diseased and unclean consequences went to the heart of his pathology. Whatever the truth of the matter, long absences and compulsive and reckless infidelity were not a recipe for a happy marriage and Claudia divorced him in 1972.

Ridgway was married and divorced three times. A few of his former wives and partners would later report that his appetite for sex was insatiable, and he particularly enjoyed outdoor sex with a risk of discovery. He was also a lifelong user of sex workers, even when he was in superficially content and monogamous sexual relationships. Despite this, and even when he was actively murdering dozens of young women, he also remained a committed religious believer.

Ridgway began his most intense period of killing in 1982, the year after he was divorced from his second wife, Marcia Brown, with whom he had a son. He would later tell the court that he'd killed so many he'd been unable to keep a count. His typical modus operandi was to pick up sex workers or vulnerable young women or children on State Route 99, generally known as the Pacific Highway and running north to south from Everett to Tacoma via Seattle in Washington State. He would play the safe family man, showing his victims a photograph of his young son, then engage in paid sexual activity. At some point during the sex act, he would strangle his victims to death either with his forearm or with a ligature.

He claimed to have killed most of his victims in his home, the departure of his wife and child giving him more leeway to kill at his leisure. Their remains were left in various rural locations in South King County, Washington State, and he developed a habit of clustering numerous bodies together in favoured sites. He told authorities that his habit of returning to these sites for necrophiliac gratification was a calculated act of self-preservation: by reusing an existing victim, he limited the risk of arrest that came with stalking fresh prey. He also deliberately cross-contaminated bodies with items from other dump sites and transported some of his victims across state lines into Oregon, in a bid to confuse the authorities.

A particularly harrowing aspect of the Gary Ridgway story is the number of women killed after he was identified as a likely serial killer. One salient issue is that, while DNA evidence was available, the science of DNA analysis was still a work in progress. Another much-discussed issue is that not enough use was made of spray paint found on the remains of Ridgway's first known victim and the seven that followed. It has been alleged that techniques of microscopic analysis available in the early 1980s could have linked crime-scene samples to materials used in Ridgway's job as a painter of commercial vehicles.

Ridgway was arrested in both 1982 and 2001 for charges related to his use of sex workers. He was identified as a person of interest by the Green River Task Force in 1983; in 1984 he was interviewed by law enforcement and passed a lie-detector test with flying colours; and in 1987 detectives took hair and saliva samples from him. In a twist that has inspired many works of serial-killer fiction, Ted Bundy (see Chapter Four) was consulted on the Green River manhunt and offered an ultimately accurate prediction that the suspect was in the habit of returning to his dump sites to indulge in necrophilia. According to *The New York Times*, Bundy got the ball rolling by writing to Detective Dave Reichart from death row, saying, inter alia, "don't ask me why I believe I'm an expert in this area, just accept that I am and we'll start from there."

Despite a huge investment of time and resources, neither federal nor local law enforcement could find a way to stop

Ridgway's killings and successfully charge him. Nearly two decades would pass before he would be brought to justice, two decades in which many in both law enforcement and the wider community knew that Ridgway was one of the USA's most prolific serial killers. Despite being busy with solicitation, risky sex, murder, necrophilia, evading justice and full-time work, Ridgway still found time for romance. He began dating Judith Mawson in 1985 and married her in 1988. It is believed that the pace of Ridgway's killing declined sharply after he married for the third time, and Judith later told the press that she believed she'd saved lives by making him happy. She also added that she'd found bare floorboards in his house when she moved in, presumably because he'd used the carpet to dispose of bodies. He had also made spurious claims to be working early shifts when, in all likelihood, he was busy stalking and murdering.

In 2001, DNA technology had advanced to the point where samples taken from Ridgway in 1987 could be analyzed and matched with crime-scene semen samples. He was still working as a vehicle painter at a Kenworth truck factory when he was arrested. DNA evidence underpinned the first four crimes with which Ridgway was charged, those being the murders of Marcia Chapman, 31, Opal Mills, 16, Cynthia Hinds, 17, and Carol Christensen, 21. Three more murders were added to the indictment following belated microscopic analysis of spray paint that had been used by Ridgway at the Kenworth factory at the relevant time – those of Wendy Coffield, 16, Debra Bonner, 23, and Debra Estes, 15.

Ridgway would inflict an agonizing dilemma on King County's prosecutor. They could certainly prosecute him for seven murders and seek the death penalty. If, however, they wished to discover the fates of dozens of other murder victims, and give closure to their families, then the death penalty would have to be taken off the table. In 2003, Ridgway pleaded guilty to 48 murder charges, having agreed to help law enforcement to trace the remains of his victims and give them a full picture of his offending in exchange for his life.

In a gruelling five-month marathon of investigative interviews, Ridgway confessed to 48 murders. He also claimed to have killed a total of between 65 and 71 victims. He may well have been in earnest when he claimed to have lost track of numbers; it is also possible that he withheld details as a thrilling, final act of sadism. At the time of writing, Ridgway remains incarcerated at the Washington State Penitentiary and is likely to die there.

Ridgway is generally regarded as a mission-oriented killer because of his single-minded commitment to murdering female sex workers. It is striking that, while he echoed his father by indulging in moral indignation about the presence of sex workers on his neighbourhood's streets, seeing them as a form of moral pollution, he also solicited and paid for intercourse with those women. There was a sharp-edged moral dilemma at work in Ridgway's mind: he needed a certain kind of sexual gratification and passionately despised that need. It is a shame that he lacked the courage and clarity of mind to see where the ultimate problem lay. Had he inflicted lethal violence on the ultimate source of this moral imbroglio, himself, then dozens of cruel murders might have been avoided.

JOSEPH PAUL FRANKLIN: GOD'S OWN SNIPER

Between 1977 and 1980, Joseph Paul Franklin murdered up to 22 people in various states of the USA and attempted to murder six others. He is regarded both as a domestic terrorist and as an archetypal mission-oriented serial killer. He was motivated directly and explicitly by his commitment to white supremacism, and he described his serial killing as a "mission".

Born James Clayton Vaughn Jr, Franklin was born in 1950 in Mobile, Alabama, USA. His father, James Clayton Vaughn Sr, was a former soldier who abandoned his family when Franklin was eight years old. His mother, Helen Rau Vaughn, was a homebuilder of German origin known for her strictness. Both parents were physically abusive and negligent in their care of their four children. Regular beatings could be expected, whereas regular meals could not.

As a result of neglect, Franklin lagged behind his peers intellectually, physically and emotionally. He appears to have been no more than an inconvenience to his family and it is therefore unsurprising that he was receptive to offers of meaning and belonging from elsewhere. In his teens, an interest in evangelical Christianity morphed into something darker and he joined the National Socialist White People's Party and the Ku Klux Klan. Both of these organizations promote a variety of extreme right-wing ideas and, broadly speaking, promote the idea that white Protestants of European descent are racially distinct from and superior to people of other races and cultures. They also hold that their ideas have a mandate from God.

The psychologist Abraham Maslow is best remembered for his hierarchy of needs, a model of human motivation usually visualized as a pyramid. At the broad base of the pyramid are basic human needs, such as food, water and security. At the tapering middle levels are psychological needs, such as meaningful relationships and sources of self-esteem. At the narrow summit of the model is self-actualization, a term initially coined by psychiatrist Kurt Goldstein. Self-actualization represents the pinnacle of human fulfilment; by finding rewarding, creative, impactful ways to live their life, a person can exceed setbacks and limitations and find deep contentment and meaning.

Franklin's journey might be explained by Maslow's hierarchy. He started as an unwanted, neglected teenager with poor self-esteem and a need to belong; through struggle and devotion, he became a self-actualized domestic terrorist with a sense of divine purpose. He adopted the nom de guerre by which he is best known, Joseph Paul Franklin, to reflect his new purpose and identity. In doing so, he nodded to two very different characters: Paul Joseph Goebbels, Adolf Hitler's propaganda chief, and Benjamin Franklin, US polymath and Founding Father.

In the early 1920s, Adolf Hitler spent time in prison following an attempted coup. He passed the time by writing a now infamous book. He wanted to call it *Viereinhalb Jahre (des Kampfes) gegen Lüge, Dummheit und Feigheit* (*Four and a Half Years (of Struggle) Against Lies, Stupidity and Cowardice*). That title reflected the writer's peevish, vindictive and febrile disposition and was shortened to the dignified, sober and more saleable *Mein Kampf* (*My Struggle*) at the behest of its publisher. It is tempting to imagine how history might have differed had Hitler's unhinged original title been retained. It is also tempting to wonder what would have become of Franklin had he not picked up the book in the late 1960s and been inspired to stop talking about a race war and actually begin one.

In the early 1970s, Franklin embraced his new family, spending time with significant figures in the white-supremacist movement including David Duke and Don Black. He also picked up useful skills from his far-right family, not least marksmanship; some of his crimes would be distinguished by accurate shooting over long distances. In the late 1970s, Franklin began his race war in earnest, targeting Jewish and black people, whom he considered racially unclean. He would later maintain that he had been a soldier fighting for the survival of the white race, and held a particular animus against interracial couples, whom he believed had sullied or diluted racial purity. This self-appointed job did not come with a salary or benefits, so Franklin robbed banks to fund himself. He also occasionally donated blood, a voluntary undertaking in many countries but routinely a paid one in the USA at that time; this would become significant later.

On 29 July 1977, Franklin attacked the Beth Sholom Synagogue in Chattanooga, Tennessee, with an incendiary device that, fortunately, killed nobody. His ignorance may have saved lives, for he made this attempt late on a Friday after the worshippers had left. In Judaism, the Sabbath is the divinely ordained day of rest and runs from sunset on Friday to sunset on Saturday. He was not deterred, however. On 7 August in the car park of a mall in Madison, Wisconsin, Franklin shot dead a couple, Alphonse Manning Jr and Toni Schwenn. A few months later, on 8 October 1977, he ambushed several people at the Brith Sholom Kneseth Israel Synagogue in St Louis, Missouri, shooting to death 42-year-old Gerald Gordon and wounding two other men.

On 6 March 1978, Franklin committed the crime that would later garner the most media attention. Infamous and wealthy publisher, libertarian and pornographer Larry Flynt and his lawyer Gene Reeves were in Lawrenceville, Georgia, to contest a lawsuit. Franklin shot both men on the street with a hunting rifle, leaving Reeves seriously wounded and Flynt using a wheelchair and in permanent pain. Franklin had been inspired to kill Flynt while browsing an edition of the pornographic magazine *Hustle* that featured an interracial photo shoot. It is of note that the concept of miscegenation – the idea that the mixing of supposedly pure bloodlines is sinful, traitorous or taboo – held a particular fascination for him.

Franklin later returned to Chattanooga, Tennessee, where on 29 July 1978 he used a shotgun to shoot Bryan Tatum and Nancy Hilton, killing Bryan and seriously wounding Nancy. A full year passed before the next murder that could be definitively attributed to Franklin. On 12 July 1979 in Doraville, Georgia, Harold McIver, the Black manager of a fast-food restaurant, was shot dead through his window from 140 m (460 ft) away. He had piqued Franklin's ire just by routinely interacting with white women, offering a window into Franklin's modus operandi. Franklin seems to have drifted from state to state, watching for ordinary social interactions that violated his ideological creed and then planning short-range ambushes or long-range assassinations.

On 21 October in Oklahoma City, Oklahoma, Franklin shot dead a married couple, Jesse Taylor and Marion Bresette. There was another hiatus until the spring of 1980, from which point the pace of Franklin's killings escalated. On 29 May 1980, civil rights activist Vernon Jordan was shot and wounded in Fort Wayne, Indiana, and his crime was simply to have been seen with a white woman. On 8 June, he murdered two children, Darrell Lane, 14, and Dante Brown, 13, in Cincinnati, Ohio. A week later, on 15 June, he shot and killed a couple, Arthur Smothers and Kathleen Mikula, in Johnstown, Pennsylvania, with a long-range rifle. On 25 June, he killed two hitchhikers, Nancy Santomero and Vicki Durian, with a handgun because he formed the impression that one of them had a Black boyfriend. His final confirmed murder victims were Ted Fields and David Martin, both shot dead in Salt Lake City, Utah, on 20 August 1980.

Shortly after his final murders, Franklin was detained on suspicion of firearms offences in Kentucky. He managed to flee but his car was seized and it yielded evidence that he had been responsible for the so-called sniper killings, along with numerous insights into his lifestyle, including his habit of donating blood for money. Alerts were issued to blood banks to be on the lookout for a man with distinctive white-supremacist tattoos and this led to Franklin's arrest in Florida in October 1980.

Franklin's judicial cavalcade proceeded at a leisurely pace over the next two decades as various jurisdictions brought their own charges against him. He was convicted of eight murders and is likely to have committed at least 14 more in addition to numerous offences of wounding and robbery. In November 2013, 33 years after his arrest in Florida, Franklin was executed by lethal injection in Bonne Terre, Missouri.

Franklin no doubt saw himself as a man of principle at the time of his murders – and in this regard was an archetypal mission-oriented killer – although he later claimed to have educated himself out of racism during decades of incarceration. Another man of stubbornly held principles, and one whose life had been blighted by Franklin, protested against Franklin's execution. Speaking to the BBC's *Newsnight* programme in 2013, Larry Flynt said: "I'm opposed to the death penalty... if the death penalty was a deterrent, I could support it. I would like to inflict the same kind of punishment on [Franklin] as he did on me... it's just that I don't think the government should be in the business of killing people."

SAEED HANAEI: THE HOLY SPIDER

Quoted in the UK's *The Guardian* newspaper in 2003, a 14-year-old boy, Ali Hanaei, spoke with pride of his father's mission to cleanse his nation of the "corrupt of the Earth". "If they kill him tomorrow," he added, "dozens will replace him". Ali was the son of Saeed Hanaei, a serial killer who murdered at least 16 women in Mashhad, Iran, between 2000 and 2001.

Saeed Hanaei was explicitly and unambiguously a mission-oriented killer, whose pathology led him to deliberately and systematically target women he considered immoral, supposedly for religious reasons. What makes his case unusual is that his self-appointed mission met with vocal, ideological approval from a powerful minority in his country. Also quoted in *The Guardian*, Ansar-e Hezbollah, a semi-official, ultra-conservative group of Iranian paramilitaries, attributed the murders to declining female morality, and said: "It is likely that what happened in Mashhad... could be repeated in Tehran."

Hanaei was born in 1962 and endured an unhappy childhood at the hands of his disturbed mother, whose abuses included scratching, gouging and biting his flesh. As a young man, he volunteered to fight in the Iran–Iraq War (1980 to 1988) and, although there is no account of what he experienced in that conflict, he later claimed that his murders were a continuation of his commitment to defend his country. At the turn of the twenty-first century, Hanaei lived in Mashhad, worked in the building industry and was married with three children.

Mashhad is Iran's most populous city after Tehran and is home to more than three million people. It lies in the semi-arid north-west of Iran, close to its border with Uzbekistan. Mashhad attracts both religious pilgrims, who travel to visit the Imam Reza shrine, and all the hustle, bustle and vices of any large city. It is of note that opium addiction is unusually prevalent in Iran. The United Nations Office on Drugs and Crime (UNODC) estimated in 2015 that, globally speaking, Iran had the second-worst opium-addiction problem and the highest per-capita rate of heroin and opium addiction. One significant factor in this is Iran's proximity to the poppy fields of Afghanistan and Pakistan and its long and porous eastern borders.

Hanaei was supposedly inspired to begin his cleansing of the streets of Mashhad when a man addressed his wife as though she were a sex worker. It goes to the heart of his pathology, and to Iran's institutional attitude to women, that he blamed women for leading men astray rather than men for desiring, harassing, soliciting and harming women. He is also unlikely to have considered other causes of social breakdown, including opium dependency. Hanaei became known as the Spider for the manner in which he trapped his prey. He worked as a contractor by day, and in the evening, while his wife and children were at prayers, he would lure women to the family home, throttle them to death, remove their remains and dump them, then return and tidy up ready to greet his family. His modus operandi included strangling his victims with a scarf, covering his victims head to toe in their chadors – the full-body female garment common in many Muslim countries – then dumping them at roadsides or in sewers.

Hanaei's first known victim was 30-year-old Afsaneh Karimpour, killed on 7 August 2000 leaving a nine-year-old girl orphaned. His killings tended to be clustered together, possibly reflecting work or family commitments. Hanaei's first three murders, for example, all took place within a week of each other. The last of 16 known victims was Zahra Dadkhosravi, whose remains were found in August 2001. All those killed were dismissively referred to as "street women" by Hanaei, and, in an unsettling echo of the UK's Yorkshire Ripper case, there was an assumption in some quarters of Iranian society that they had all plied immoral trades and were thereby responsible – partly or wholly – for their own fate. Hanaei claimed to have attacked only sex workers and described them as a "waste of blood".

Saeed Hanaei was arrested in late 2001 and was surprized to find that Iran's hardliners didn't have quite enough influence to save him from conviction and a death sentence. The self-appointed Holy Spider was hanged at dawn in Mashhad Prison on 8 April 2002. Even in a hard-line theocracy, it seems, unsanctioned vigilantism cannot be tolerated and violence in the name of God must remain the state's prerogative.

Intriguingly, Hanaei was not thought to have been a particularly conservative or fundamentalist religious believer. Although it cannot be confirmed, he may well have been as prone to vice as many of his compatriots. Stripped of his ideological baggage, Hanaei may have been every bit as pathologically driven, morally vacuous and murderously misogynistic as Peter Sutcliffe in the UK or Mikhail Popkov in Russia. It may be that the rhetoric of Iranian theocracy gave this warped and vicious killer a divine moral pretext.

Perhaps those in Iran who applauded Hanaei's actions should have stopped to ponder whether his arrogating God's power of judgement to himself, and actively enjoying the taking of human life, could ever be considered rational or moral.

MADELEINE MOUTON: THE BERTHELOT POISONER

The guillotine is an efficient tool of execution. A vertical, slotted wooden assembly holds the head of the condemned face down in a pillory at the base. At the top of the assembly, a sharp, angled and weighted blade is suspended. When the blade is released, gravity, carpentry, metallurgy, flesh and bone all come together in a fraction of a second and a head is sundered from a body. The guillotine has become symbolic of the Reign of Terror, a phase of the French Revolution during which tens of thousands were killed in organized mass public executions and other massacres.

It is thus surprising that the guillotine was a product of the Enlightenment and was intended to make judicial homicide quick and painless. In terms of human suffering, it certainly compared favourably to pre-Enlightenment execution methods, which ranged from slow crushing to hanging, drawing and quartering. Execution by guillotine has, at the time of writing, ceased, but was routinely used within living memory. France was the last country to use a guillotine in earnest, decapitating kidnapper, rapist and murderer Hamida Djandoubi in 1977. Earlier in the twentieth century, one obscure wartime serial killer also kept an appointment with Madame Guillotine.

Madeleine Mouton fatally poisoned seven people in Sidi Bel Abbès, Algeria, between 1943 and 1944, and attempted to poison four more. She was detained in 1944, tried in 1947 and in 1948 became the penultimate French woman to be executed by guillotine. The guillotine that took the life of Madeleine Mouton took more lives during the Algerian War of Independence (1954–1962), a bloody struggle by which Algeria won independence from France. It now stands as a macabre exhibit in the Central Military Museum in Algiers.

Madeleine Mouton was born Madeleine Maxence Le Veller in Normandy, France, in 1910. Her mother left her father, who had alcoholism, when Madeleine was ten, but she is known to have attended school until the age of 14. As a school child, Madeleine developed habits that initially seemed merely eccentric. She persistently claimed an aristocratic heritage and somehow acquired an empty violin case and carried it everywhere in the hope that she would be taken for a musician. It is not known what happened in Madeleine's formative years to make her self-esteem so reliant on fantasy, but the compulsion towards self-aggrandizing lies would come to define her. She allegedly tried to kill herself at the age of 17 by drinking petrol; whether this attempt was in earnest or to sustain a public façade is moot.

Madeleine married Clément Mouton in 1929 and was serially unfaithful to him, possibly for the frisson of deception or fantasy. They had their first child in 1933 and at some point before the Second World War Clément joined the Mobile Gendarmerie, a paramilitary part of French law enforcement then used to keep order in France's overseas territories. In 1940, Clément secured a transfer to what was at the time French Algeria. What prompted this move is not known, but the first year of the Second World War had been catastrophic for France. When Nazi Germany invaded and defeated France in the spring of 1940, France's government and territory were both fractured. The Free French government existed only in exile in London, while the north and west of France were occupied and harshly repressed by Germany. Southern France and territories including Corsica and Algeria were not occupied, because they were administered by Vichy France, a collaborationist regime friendly to Nazi Germany.

For the Mouton family, then, a move to unoccupied Algeria from Nazi-occupied northern France may have had much to recommend it. Madeleine, however, was not made for calm contentment. The family first lived in Constantine in north-eastern Algeria, where she indulged in multiple extramarital affairs and spectacular alcoholic binges on the grounds that the climate did not suit her. She also lost a child shortly after a traumatic birth.

The nature of the relationship between the Moutons is uncertain, but it is known that Clément repeatedly transferred from one settlement to another in a bid to escape both his wife's reputation for promiscuity and high living and his reputation as a weak husband or a cuckold. By 1942, they were stationed at Berthelot near Sidi Bel Abbès, their fourth posting, where Madeleine's unreformed and brazen misbehaviour saw her barred from living in police barracks.

In 1941 and 1942, she had conceived and given birth to two more children.

The precise details of Madeleine's lifestyle are hazy but she certainly didn't live like a stereotypical 1940s housewife. She insisted on satisfying her needs for sex, romance, alcohol and adventure, and one of her conquests was her husband's boss. She frequently disappeared for days at a time to Sidi Bel Abbès and financed her lifestyle with multiple loans despite the fact that she lacked the means to service them, much less redeem them.

By 1943, the tenor of expat gossip in Berthelot had changed from amused disbelief to horrified concern. A number of painful deaths aroused the suspicions of local medics, who concurred that acute poisoning was the only explanation. Even before the Mobile Gendarmerie was called upon to investigate, the small community had begun to look upon Madeleine Mouton's eccentricities with less indulgent eyes.

The poisonings had begun in January 1943. While Madeleine was staying with the Leroux family, the lady of the house became gravely ill and died, while her husband survived despite similar symptoms. The local expat community raised 2,400 francs cash to support the Lerouxs' daughter, Micheline; Madeleine misappropriated this sum while borrowing another 4,000 francs from a Madame Lamasse, purportedly to pay for Micheline's tuition. What Madeleine did with the cash remains a mystery, but high living and a long line of creditors offer a possible explanation.

In April 1943, Madame Lamasse's mother-in-law died in similar circumstances to Madame Leroux, followed in December by a Monsieur Bene. Of the various incidents in which people had been rendered gravely ill or had died of poisoning, Madeleine Mouton was the common denominator: all of the victims had received her solicitous care and friendship. Her own husband, Clément, had been poisoned and survived, while their ten-month-old child succumbed. When Clément's colleagues from the Mobile Gendarmerie investigated, they discovered that Madeleine had bought a quantity of sodium arsenite, supposedly for pest control.

Used primarily then and now as a pesticide, sodium arsenite – a compound of sodium, arsenic and oxygen – is highly carcinogenic. Mere skin contact with the substance can produce symptoms including convulsions, lowered blood pressure, vomiting, diarrhoea and burns. If ingested, the compound will attack the nervous system and cause muscular weakness, reduced sensation, paralysis and ultimately death. Sodium arsenite has no odour but tastes either salty or like garlic with a metallic edge; it is therefore possible to introduce it into a victim's meals without drawing undue attention.

Despite the fact that she was married to a police officer, and had been having an affair with at least one senior officer, Madeleine Mouton was arrested in April 1944 and confessed to four of her murders. While detained in Algiers in October 1944, she cultivated a close friendship with a jailer, seemingly with a view to "pleading the belly" – receiving special treatment or mercy by reason of pregnancy – but her plan foundered. While she did get to spend time in a maternity ward, the pregnancy didn't materialize.

Mouton may have been a mission-oriented serial killer. While there are few detailed insights into her underlying pathology, it is clear that she was willing to kill repeatedly and without remorse to facilitate her lifestyle. She may have wanted to rid herself of those who might have punctured her fantastical, romantic and hedonistic existence. It may be that a few died in the hope that some of Mouton's debts would die with them or so that their money could be misappropriated. Others may have been poisoned simply because they were tedious or inconvenient. Perhaps murderer was just a role she tried on for size and enjoyed.

While Madeleine's actions were too coherent and consistent to suggest clinical delusion sufficient for a successful insanity plea, they may have been just one facet of an all-consuming, pathological need to present a grandiose version of herself to the world. Even in detention, she wasn't content to be seen as herself: she convinced staff and inmates that she was a heroic political prisoner, locked up for voicing admiration for Vichy France's leader, Philippe Pétain. In 1945, a court psychiatrist reported that Mouton was a heavy drinker but was otherwise compos mentis and capable of forming criminal intent.

While the guillotine was undoubtedly less cruel than the medieval implements it replaced, the terror of any process of execution should not be underestimated. When Madeleine Mouton was woken at dawn on 10 April 1948 to be introduced to Madame Guillotine, she was under the impression that her sentence was about to be commuted to life imprisonment. When the situation was starkly explained to her, she fainted, and a doctor was summoned to ensure that she was conscious and alert when her head was parted from her body.

PEDRO RODRIGUES FILHO: THE BRAZILIAN PUNISHER

The fear of crime and the exploits of heroic crime fighters and dastardly villains are fertile ground for a remarkable range of art and entertainment. One of many subgenres of crime fiction explores the antics of vigilantes, fictional heroes and anti-heroes who tire of ineffectual or corrupt law enforcement and take matters into their own hands. The most famous of these are costumed superheroes with varying degrees of gadgetry and moral inhibition.

The principal superpower of the DC Comics character Batman is that he is a billionaire, and he scrupulously avoids killing his foes. At the other end of the spectrum is Marvel Comics character The Punisher, a working-class former soldier who metes out torture and death to murderous criminals. The twenty-first century brought another vision of the vigilante archetype to the world's bookshelves and TV screens: the well-intentioned and socially beneficial serial killer in the person of Dexter Morgan, title character in Jeff Lindsay's *Dexter* novels and their TV spin-offs. Perhaps the Dexter franchise's most striking feature is that it was inspired by a prolific real-life serial killer who claimed to target only criminals.

Pedro Rodrigues Filho, known by nicknames including the Brazilian Punisher, Killer Petey and Pedrinho Matador, killed at least 71 people in Brazil between 1968 and 2007. Rodrigues was born in 1954 to a farming family in Santa Rita do Sapucaí near Minas Gerais in the south-east of Brazil. Little is known about his early years but he claimed that his skull was bruised in utero as a result of his abusive father kicking his pregnant mother. He also claimed that he discovered his innate need to kill at the age of 13 while fighting with his cousin. The other boy fell into an agricultural press and Filho gave serious thought to watching him die before changing his mind and saving him.

In 1968 at the age of 14, Rodrigues shot dead both the deputy mayor and the school security guard in Santa Rita do Sapucaí. Rodrigues's father, also a school security guard, had been sacked by the deputy mayor on suspicion of theft, for which the murdered guard had, it was believed, actually been responsible. In the manner of a violent revenge movie, Rodrigues exacted rough justice with his grandfather's shotgun, then fled and lived the life of an outlaw.

Rodrigues moved to the populous São Paulo municipality of Mogi das Cruzes but did not keep a low profile for long. He terrorized local crime gangs, robbing drug dens and killing traffickers. This created a power vacuum in local gangs that he proceeded to fill. He was then supposedly obliged to kill rivals to consolidate his power, and the cycle of violence kept churning. During his reign of terror, he met Maria Aparecida Olympia, the love of his life, but she was murdered by a rival gang while pregnant with his child. This impelled

Rodrigues, still in his mid-teens, to embark on a scorched-earth campaign; over time, he found and murdered anyone and everyone connected with the rival gang that had killed his lover.

Rodrigues's wings were finally clipped when he was arrested in 1973 at the age of 18. He was convicted of 71 murders and sentenced to a prison term of 126 years, but a statutory limitation on sentencing saw him released in 2007 at the age of 34. Even inside the system, Rodrigues seized upon at least one opportunity for rough justice. It is alleged that, while sharing a prison transport vehicle, he killed his fellow passenger without causing any kind of commotion. When the prison officers eventually opened the vehicle and found one living prisoner rather than two, Rodrigues explained that the other man was dead because he was a rapist.

Rodrigues committed the vast majority of his murders while under the age of 18 and would spend very little of his adult life outside the Brazilian prison system. After serving yet more prison time in the 2010s for offences including serious public disorder, he embraced the twenty-first century and set up a successful YouTube channel in which he spoke out against criminality and gang culture. In March 2023 at the age of 68, Rodrigues was murdered in a drive-by shooting in Mogi das Cruzes. The relative's child he was carrying survived unscathed.

Pedro Rodrigues Filho was emphatically a mission-oriented killer. He candidly admitted that he had an innate urge to kill and he satisfied that urge prolifically but not indiscriminately. His pathology needed a moral pretext and in this respect he was not untypical. His moral code was rough and ready but tended to align loosely with the ideas of natural justice that typify fictional vigilantes. This does not, however, sanitize his actions; his code was essentially a self-certified licence to kill. Rodrigues may have considered himself a moral killer, but so did Peter Sutcliffe, Saeed Hanaei and Joseph Paul Franklin.

Whether they are fact or fiction, the stories of murderous vigilantes fascinate us because they pose provocative questions. Do we allow ourselves to enjoy and approve of murder if we happen to disapprove of the victim's moral choices? If so, what does that say about us? Might it be the case that many of us, in our secret hearts and private viewing choices, are tempted to applaud a certain kind of mission-oriented serial killer? This might explain the remarkable success of *Dexter* and other fictional vigilantes whose violent antics we find ourselves rooting for.

MARIAM SOULAKIOTIS: MOTHER RASPUTIN

It is difficult, from a modern, Western, secular standpoint, to comprehend the literal and absolutist nature of religious belief in medieval Europe. It is correspondingly hard to imagine how extraordinarily powerful medieval religious orders were, and not just in a spiritual sense. Even to the faithful in those societies, the ruthlessness with which some holy orders sought to accumulate wealth was troubling. From the extraction of tithes from labourers living in poverty to the selling of indulgences to the wealthy – crudely speaking, a scam by which the Catholic Church could erase sins or shorten time in purgatory in exchange for cold, hard cash – the church's worldly venality was remarkable. Not only did the English Reformation make Henry VIII head of his own church and free him to marry whomever he chose, but the plunder gained from dissolving the great monastic orders swelled his coffers to the tune of £1.3 million (or £1.1 billion in 2024).

Yet the medieval church didn't hold a monopoly on absolute faith and ruthless, hypocritical greed, and these traits prosper still in many walks of life. A chilling reminder of their power, however, could be found in a decidedly old-fashioned religious order in twentieth-century Greece, and in its notorious leader, the Abbess Mariam Soulakiotis. Between 1939 and 1951, Soulakiotis is alleged to have killed 177 individuals, 27 by deliberate starvation and 150 by fraud or negligence, all in pursuit of filthy lucre.

The story of the dreaded Abbess Mariam Soulakiotis has obscure and esoteric origins. It is thought that she was born Marina Soulakiotis in 1883 in Keratea, East Attica, a rural area south-east of Athens, Greece. After a period of factory work, she took holy orders and became a nun in the Greek Orthodox Church (GOC). In the 1920s, a schism developed in the GOC over the validity of religious rites performed by those in the mainstream who had adopted the Revised Julian calendar. Soulakiotis joined the Old Calendarist schismatics, a niche sect who insisted on using the old Julian calendar. Incidentally, both calendars are distinct from the Gregorian calendar used by most of the world. At first glance, it seems incomprehensible that people of faith would split their communion over such an arcane issue. However, so axiomatic was this article of faith to Soulakiotis's belief system, and so fervent was that belief, that over time she would kill for it repeatedly.

Having split from her parent church, in 1927 Soulakiotis founded the Convent of the Virgin in the Pines (also known as the Panagia Pefkovounogiatrissa Monastery) close to her home in East Attica. She was joined in this endeavour by Archbishop Matthew Karpathakis, who made their mission very clear: not only would they honour the Virgin Mary, but they also would raise the substantial sums of money that the

Old Calendarist movement needed to further its aims. Indeed, the inclusion of "pines" in the convent's title was part of a plan to exploit its picturesque, hilly location overlooking the Aegean Sea by marketing it as a TB treatment centre. It is of note that, prior to the wide-scale introduction of antibiotics in the mid-twentieth century, TB was often fatal. It is also of note that the Convent of the Virgin in the Pines offered clean air and pleasant views rather than clinical expertise.

Soulakiotis was de facto abbess of her convent from 1939 onwards. Karpathakis was frequently absent, in body and soul, for reasons ranging from fasting to penance, imprisonment, poor health and, on at least one occasion, self-mortification by staggering around under the weight of heavy metal chains in a manner reminiscent of the ghost of Jacob Marley in Charles Dickens's *A Christmas Carol*. While Soulakiotis may have set up the monastery as a joint endeavour with the old and ailing bishop, she came to control both it and him totally, even to the point, it is alleged, of preventing him from healing the schism with the GOC before his death in 1950.

Soulakiotis did, however, go to extraordinary lengths to fulfil her promise to put the Old Calendarists on a firm financial footing. One easily overlooked aspect of her grim fundraising campaign is that it coincided with the Second World War and its repercussions. During the winter of 1940 into 1941, Greece fought off an Italian invasion. From April 1941, Nazi Germany invaded and conquered Greece and it endured a repressive occupation until October 1944, by which time 250,000 had died, with Greek Jews almost exterminated. The country then endured civil war between 1946 and 1949. Even in these circumstances, Soulakiotis plied her trade energetically. Even against this backdrop, her crimes would stand out.

Soulakiotis's modus operandi was single-minded and well organized. She prepared by establishing complete control over the convent's nuns and monks, then, from 1940, she sent the monks on scouting trips around war-torn Greece. They sought out wealthy families and individuals who might be ripe for religious conversion and persuaded them to travel to the Convent of the Virgin in the Pines. Once there, they would be held under lock and key and tortured, starved, beaten and exposed to TB until they agreed to sign over their assets to the convent. While it is difficult to accurately value the assets obtained in this manner, it is known that Soulakiotis acquired titles to at least 300 farms and homes alongside jewellery and cash. Of greater import is the fact that at least 27 died during this process of extortion by torture.

It is likely that the Greek authorities received numerous complaints from concerned relatives, but the intervention of the FBI and the international media may have compelled them to take a closer look at Soulakiotis. Simela Spyrides, 18, a US national of Greek birth, went missing in 1949. The FBI had established that the young woman had been drawn to the infamous convent by a nun, the same nun who had been so committed to her cause that she had travelled to the USA to collect a financial gift. In December 1950, an impressive force of 85 police officers accompanied by numerous public officials raided the Convent of the Virgin in the Pines. They liberated 36 children and an unspecified number of wretched, half-starved, half-naked women found tied up in a basement. The officers had to fight tooth and nail to free the convent's guests, as Soulakiotis had attracted at least 400 acolytes to her personal cult.

Greek law enforcement planned to prosecute Soulakiotis, together with 13 monks and nuns who'd done her bidding, for multiple murders. They also planned to charge them with manslaughter for the deaths of 150 individuals who had sought treatment for TB but who had died due to a combination of incompetence, fraudulent marketing and fanatical religious asceticism. Soulakiotis denied all charges against her, apparently convinced that she had done God's will and that any suggestion to the contrary was a diabolical fiction. She died in 1954 at the age of 71 before she could be held to account for more than a fraction of the horrors she'd perpetrated.

Soulakiotis was a clear-cut mission-oriented serial killer in as much as she tortured and killed a specific category of victims with a clear, consistent objective and in a highly organized manner. It is harder to form a more profound view of her motivation and pathology. Was her warped religious creed so narrow and so fixed that she sincerely believed her actions would win her a seat at God's right hand in the hereafter? Was there some formative trauma that instilled a pathological need to control the beliefs of some while harming and impoverishing outsiders? While the acquisition of wealth was interwoven with her cruelty, the extent to which she used that wealth for luxury, self-indulgence or anything other than the furtherance of her personal cult is moot.

Soulakiotis was nicknamed Mother Rasputin by contemporary media, a reference to the famously toxic mystic of pre-revolutionary Russia. Remarkably, however, Soulakiotis is still allegedly venerated as the saintly and innocent Mariam of Keratea by current members of her religious order. It is to be hoped that they revere her in the belief that she is innocent, rather than because faith trumps basic morality. It should also be borne in mind that after the unholy convent was raided in 1950, when its prisoners and torture victims were freed, and when Mother Rasputin and her lieutenants were arrested, its resident cultists marched in protest and threatened to kidnap another victim unless God's will were done and their leaders restored to them.

It seems unlikely that Soulakiotis would have had much truck with avant-garde philosophers like Albert Camus, and, even if she knew of the Myth of Sisyphus, it probably didn't feature prominently in Old Calendarist dogma. In the case of Mother Rasputin, the mission that oriented her killings had a gloss of piety, and she may have believed in earnest that God approved of her actions. Strip away the religious trappings, however, and Soulakiotis shared the underlying pathology of any other mission-oriented killer. She had an all-consuming purpose and she would see it through, without regard to reason, morality or human suffering.

CHAPTER THREE:

HEDONISTIC SERIAL KILLERS

THE MIND OF A HEDONISTIC KILLER

In the dictionary, hedonism is defined most simply as the pursuit of pleasure, with an emphasis on sensual rather than intellectual satisfaction. In psychology, the definition adds an element of social reciprocity, whereby hedonism entails us behaving towards each other in a way that maximizes the chance of pleasure and minimizes the chance of pain. If unchecked egotism is added to the mix, hedonism becomes transactional, expressed in the idea that people will offer assistance only if they stand to benefit equally in return.

In philosophy, hedonism becomes a far more nuanced concept. In one school of thought, axiological hedonism, the pursuit of pleasure is the sole source of intrinsic value – that is, it is the only route towards the only thing that is actually worth having. While the debate on the nature and moral status of hedonism has been ongoing for thousands of years and is unlikely to be settled any time soon, some of those who have embraced its most crude and egotistical definition happen to be some of modern history's most appalling serial killers.

The egotistical, selfish gratification of personal desires with utter indifference to the lives of others is what defines these killers. For visionary killers, the suffering of others is either irrelevant or incomprehensible. For mission-oriented killers, such suffering is acceptable collateral damage in the pursuit of a greater purpose. For *power-oriented killers, suffering is a means of expressing dominance and control. What marks out hedonistic killers is that the suffering of the victim is not merely incidental – it is in fact the entire point of the whole murderous enterprise.*

This should chill the reader. Hedonistic serial killers murder because, first and foremost, they thoroughly enjoy it. The killings are often intimate and hands-on because the process of murder and its effects on the victim are savoured. Slow methods of killing and prolonged torture appeal to such killers because painting the canvas of their imaginations with a rich palette of pain is the ultimate goal. Their concept of hedonism is wholly transactional: the pleasure they experience is intense in direct proportion to the pain and fear they inflict on their victims.

Ian Brady and Myra Hindley made sport of torturing children to death and recorded one such ordeal for their own listening pleasure. They also dabbled in philosophy to find a shallow, fraudulent moral gloss for their predilections. Fred and Rose West sexualized their prolonged torture and murder sessions, making them a normal and ultimately banal part of their endless search for new thrills. Rodney Alcala sought to garnish his enjoyment by appearing on and winning a TV dating show while he was actively hunting victims. For Kenneth Bianchi, kidnapping, raping, torturing, killing and indulging in post-mortem degradation was an extreme sport to be enjoyed with a like-minded buddy.

In each of the cases you're about to read, nothing in this world mattered more to the killers than the sparks of ecstasy they got from torture, rape and murder. No amount of pain, terror, pleading, blood, horror and wasted human life could tip the scales against the murderous egotist's appetite for the thrill kill.

IAN BRADY AND MYRA HINDLEY: THE MOORS MURDERERS

On 12 July 1963, in what is now Greater Manchester, UK, 25-year-old Ian Brady and 20-year-old Myra Hindley abducted, sexually assaulted and murdered 16-year-old Pauline Reade. Pauline's mutilated remains were recovered decades later from a shallow grave on bleak moorland. Until their arrest in October 1965, Brady and Hindley claimed the lives of five young people between the ages of ten and 17.

Brady and Hindley were convicted of three murders in May 1966 and sentenced to life imprisonment. The circumstances of the other two murders would come to light later. But for the fact that the UK suspended capital punishment in 1965 and then abolished it in 1998, Brady and Hindley would in all probability have been hanged. They were textbook hedonistic serial killers: they were seekers of grim thrills, drawn to murder and cruelty by a desire for excitement, escapism and sexual gratification. Their crimes were defined by intimate physical and sexual abuse, some of it prolonged.

The county of Greater Manchester was created in 1974 and comprises a number of populous urban boroughs centred on the City of Manchester in the north-west of England. Nicknamed Cottonopolis in the nineteenth century, metropolitan Manchester in the 1960s still bore the hallmarks of the Industrial Revolution, which had brought both grandeur and squalor at either end of the social spectrum. Manchester Town Hall is a vast neo-Gothic monument to civic pride, but it was soot-stained by industry and the hazy view from its spire was dominated by endless ranks of tenement housing for poorly paid workers. On a particularly clear day, however, one might glimpse Saddleworth Moor to the north-east, part of the Pennine Hills that hem in this great conurbation on its eastern flank.

Ian Brady was not a native of Manchester; he came from the Gorbals, a low-income, crowded, working-class area of Glasgow, Scotland. Brady never knew his father, his single mother struggled to cope and he spent much of his childhood in the care of another family. According to *The Independent* and other newspapers, Brady bragged that from the age of ten he'd tortured and killed various animals. It has been speculated that Brady was afflicted by zoosadism, a form of paraphilia whereby the subject derives intense pleasure from inflicting pain on animals up to the point of death. As mentioned in a previous chapter, psychiatrist J. M. Macdonald suggested in 1963 that zoosadism, alongside obsessive fire-starting and bed-wetting beyond early childhood, is a predictor of serial violence.

By the age of 17, Brady had a criminal record that included housebreaking and threats of violence and he had moved with his mother to Manchester. He fared little better there and a clumsy attempt to steal lead saw him incarcerated at tough Victorian prisons in Manchester and Hull. Brady was a petty thief with a poor temper but he was emphatically not a mindless thug. If subjects captured his imagination, Brady could be an avid reader; it is unfortunate that those subjects included torture, genocide and sadomasochism.

Myra Hindley was born and brought up in the working-class Manchester borough of Gorton. Her father was a war veteran and violent person with alcoholism, notorious for inflicting violence on his wife and children and for encouraging Myra and her siblings to become violent in their own right. If Myra was beaten by other children and did not respond in kind, she would be beaten again at home.

Hindley endured a troubled, brutalizing childhood that left her morally conflicted. In her teenage years, a close male friend drowned in an abandoned reservoir and she blamed herself for not being on hand to save him. In her mid-teens, Hindley was drawn to the Roman Catholic Church and took communion. At 17, she took her first job as a clerk and became engaged, but called off the wedding plans abruptly a few months later. She may also have remembered the brutal lessons learned in early childhood; she practised judo in young adulthood but was known to play too roughly and struggled to find training partners.

Together, Brady and Hindley became more than the sum of their bad parts. The two met at Millwards Merchandise, a wholesaler of industrial chemicals in Gorton, for whom they both did clerical work. They became a couple in December 1961 when Brady was 23 and Hindley 19. Their early dates revolved around X-rated movies – films classified as containing explicit violence or sex – followed by late-night drinking sessions. They also formed a two-person book club and shared a taste for the works of Nietzsche, de Sade and Dostoevsky, as well as lurid accounts of war crimes and torture. They whiled away their lunch hours at work by narrating accounts of genocidal Nazi violence to one another, strengthening their own bond and keeping their colleagues at arm's length.

In the late 1970s, Hindley would claim in her plea for parole that Brady had powers of persuasion bordering on the supernatural. Even if she is taken at her word, Hindley was wide open to persuasion and embraced her role in the partnership with gusto. The post-arrest photograph by which she is best known features the bleached hair and heavy lipstick she used to emulate a Nazi notion of Teutonic purity. She was far from passive in planning and commissioning the pair's crimes. She passed her driving test on her fourth attempt in 1963 so that she could hire and drive a van, and she ingratiated herself with a shooting club and managed to purchase firearms, both steps taken with a view to staging violent robberies. While Brady had up to this point not amounted to much as a criminal, with Hindley he would almost make good on his plan to commit the perfect murder.

Brady became infatuated with the concept of the perfect murder around 1963, possibly as a result of reading Meyer Levin's 1956 crime novel, *Compulsion*. The novel was a fictionalized account of the infamous murder of 14-year-old Bobby Franks by Nathan Leopold and Richard Loeb in Chicago, USA, in 1924. Leopold and Loeb had infamously committed their crime as an act of egocentric vanity. It was not inspired by any specific animus against the victim, but rather by a desire to prove that their intellectual superiority should place them beyond moral or legal consequences. This murder is perhaps best known today for inspiring the 1948 Alfred Hitchcock movie, *Rope*, a chilling examination of evil famously filmed in only two takes. In criminology, Leopold, Loeb, Brady and Hindley would all come to share column inches in analyses of hedonistic serial killers.

In July 1963, Brady and Hindley shelved their robbery plans and embraced recreational murder. The pair were living together in Gorton and one summer evening after work they went out hunting. Hindley prowled the neighbourhood in a van while Brady followed on his motorcycle; Brady would flash his headlight if he saw a suitable victim. An unnamed eight-year-old girl had a lucky escape when Hindley ignored Brady's signal, having recognized the child as her mother's neighbour; whether she demurred out of squeamishness or prudence isn't certain. Hindley's scruples didn't last long and she stopped at Brady's bidding alongside 16-year-old Pauline Reade. Pauline went to school with Hindley's younger sister and knew Myra; she was wearing a pink party dress as she was on her way to a dance, and she accepted the offer of a lift.

With Pauline in the passenger seat of her van and Brady following on his motorcycle, Hindley asked the girl if she could spare the time to help search for a valuable glove lost on Saddleworth Moor. From urban Gorton to the bleak moorland above and beyond Saddleworth is not a trivial journey today, covering more than 19 km (12 mi) and taking at least half an hour by car. It is hard to say how long it would have taken more than 60 years ago, but Pauline must have felt increasingly ill at ease and far from home as the miles wore on.

What is known is that Pauline was taken onto the moor to be raped and murdered. Her throat was cut with such force that she was nearly decapitated and a necklace pushed into the wound. Hindley would claim that she had waited in the van and taken no part in the violence, only accompanying Brady immediately afterwards to watch Pauline dying. Brady would claim that Hindley had watched the violence and taken part in the sexual assault. Pauline was buried using a spade left nearby for the purpose.

Brady and Hindley would repeat this modus operandi with a few variations and improvisations. In November 1963, the pair spotted 12-year-old John Kilbride in Ashton-under-Lyne and lured him into Hindley's car with the promise of a lift and a bottle of sherry. John was taken to Saddleworth Moor, sexually assaulted, slashed, throttled and buried. In June 1964, 12-year-old Keith Bennett was spotted in Longsight and persuaded to help Hindley load boxes into her car in exchange for a lift home. He too was taken to the moors, sexually assaulted, throttled and buried.

In December 1964, Brady and Hindley were on the lookout for a new victim and new thrills. They prowled an Ancoats fairground and spotted ten-year-old Lesley Ann Downey, seemingly alone. They made a great performance of dropping shopping in front of her and asked for her help to pick it up and take it to their car. Lesley obliged and was driven to Brady and Hindley's new home at 16 Wardle Brook Avenue, Hattersley. There, she was stripped, bound, sexually abused, tortured and eventually strangled. The couple were technophiles and had invested in home-recording equipment; the resulting reel-to-reel tape of a child screaming in pain and begging for her life, accompanied by the calm, remorseless voices of Brady and Hindley, was played later in court and would haunt those who heard it. Lesley was the last to be buried on Saddleworth Moor and the last to be recovered.

Brady and Hindley finally overplayed their hand in October 1965. Brady identified a potential victim at Manchester Central train station, today a large concert venue. He persuaded 17-year-old Edward Evans to come home to Hattersley with him, introducing Hindley as his sister. At Wardle Brook Avenue, the three chatted amiably and drank wine; it is possible that Evans had been persuaded there by the possibility of sex.

Eventually, Brady decided to involve a fourth person and sent Hindley to fetch her brother-in-law, David Smith. Brady had developed an unequal friendship with Smith; Smith was supposedly awestruck by Brady, who may have enjoyed cultivating a new acolyte. Whatever the nature of this new relationship, Hindley was less than impressed, fearing that it risked exposing their activities. Brady, for his part, may have relished that risk as a new thrill. David Smith would later tell detectives that Hindley had taken him to Wardle Brook Avenue and invited him inside just in time to witness Evans's murder. He'd heard frantic screams and seen Brady strike Evans around the head with a hatchet, then choke him to death with an electrical cable. Smith was undoubtedly an accomplice in as much as he agreed to help Brady and Hindley dispose of their latest victim; it transpired that a young man's body was harder to lift than a child's. Smith got home in the early hours, broke down and confessed to his wife. He later called the police, who descended on Brady and Hindley's home, found Evans's body wrapped in plastic in a spare room and began the investigation that would ensure that both died in prison.

David Smith would become the prosecution's chief witness when Brady and Hindley were tried for murder in 1966. They tried and failed to persuade the jury that Smith had been active and complicit in the murder of Evans. Smith appears to have been treated as a witness rather than as a suspect by the police, but he was publicly stigmatized nonetheless. In 2011, he told the BBC that strangers had beaten him in the street and spat at his infant son.

The police uncovered a terrible trove of evidence at Wardle Brook Avenue, at a railway left-luggage office and on Saddleworth Moor. The pair had kept trophies, including photographs and audio recordings. Various pictures and testimony from a neighbour who'd been taken to Saddleworth Moor by the couple helped pinpoint the remains of Lesley as well as John Kilbride. One snapshot by Brady showed Hindley posing next to John's shallow grave while cuddling her dog, Puppet. The dog died when a veterinarian administered an anaesthetic while its age was being determined for evidential purposes; Hindley's anger at this accident was the only emotion she ever showed to investigating officers.

What sort of lives Brady and Hindley would have lived had they never met is a fascinating question to ponder. What is clear is that together they embodied horror beyond the sum of their cruel parts. The Moors Murderers' first and third victims, Pauline Reade and Keith Bennett, remained missing persons until 1987, when the pair admitted their murders. Both Brady and Hindley made escorted visits to Saddleworth Moor in a bid to locate the missing children. Pauline's remains were found, the pink party dress still intact. Keith's body has, to date, not been located; his mother, Winnie Johnson, fought long and hard to find her son's body but died in 2012 without succeeding.

The house at 16 Wardle Brook Avenue, Hattersley, the scene of Brady and Hindley's final two atrocities, was demolished in 1987; no matter how thoroughly it was cleaned and refurbished, the local authority could find no tenant willing to live there. The visceral aversion felt by local people towards what was, after all, a perfectly reasonable dwelling leads us to that familiar question: why? Why does anything connected with Brady and Hindley provoke revulsion, and why did they act as they did? They were first and foremost hedonistic killers, and the inescapable and intolerable conclusion is that they kidnapped, raped and tortured children not for profit, not out of delusion and not for a cause, but because they enjoyed it. There is, of course, a more complex answer to the question "why?" that encompasses formative trauma, alienation, dislocation and a warped reading of history and moral philosophy. But none of this alters the simple fact that Brady and Hindley relished death and suffering for its own sake.

The mortal remains of Keith Bennett still lie somewhere on Saddleworth Moor. A few miles to the south-west, 2.8 million inhabitants of Greater Manchester go about their quotidian business. A few miles to the north-east, the M62 motorway carries eight endless lanes of trans-Pennine commuters around the clock. Keith may as well be light years from any of them, alone in his bleak fastness of peat and heather.

EDMUND KEMPER: THE OGRE OF APTOS

Between May 1972 and April 1973, Edmund Kemper murdered one 15-year-old girl, five young women between the ages of 18 and 23, his mother and his mother's best friend. He decapitated and dismembered many of his victims and engaged in necrophilia with their remains. Prior to achieving notoriety as a paraphiliac serial killer, in 1964 at the age of 15 Kemper shot both his grandparents dead in their home.

Kemper is generally regarded as a hedonistic serial killer, motivated by paraphiliac lust and a desire to dominate and control on a viscerally intimate level up to and beyond the point of death. The extreme and gruesome coda to his offending – his tendency to return to the decaying remains of victims and sexually violate them – seems beyond rational comprehension.

Yet Kemper, like other necrophiliac serial killers, had a grim inner logic: murder meant that the victim could neither resist nor refuse and could thus be utterly possessed. Most striking of all is that, for the purposes of criminal law, Kemper was held to be sane. That aside, he is undoubtedly a psychopath, barely capable of empathy and remorse but bold, uninhibited, egotistical and devoted to his own gratification.

Edmund Kemper was born in Burbank, California, USA, in 1948 into an unhappy family. He was close to his war-veteran father, Edmund Emil Kemper Jr, and was distraught when his parents separated. At the age of 13, he moved to Montana to live with his bullying mother, who had alcoholism, Clarnell Kemper (née Strandberg). Edmund would later acquire nicknames, including Big Ed and the Ogre of Aptos, inspired by his proportions. As an adult, he would stand 2.06 m (6 ft 9 in.) tall; by the age of 15, he'd already reached 1.93 m (6 ft 4 in.) in height and was routinely mocked and humiliated for his size and awkwardness by Clarnell; she was always destined to die by Kemper's hand, but only once he had perfected his craft and shucked off his inhibitions.

In his mid-teens, Kemper ran away to California and begged his now remarried father to take him in. Shortly afterwards, Kemper was moved on yet again, this time to live with his paternal grandparents in the Sierra Nevada mountains. Any child in these circumstances, seemingly unwanted and subject to open cruelty and disdain, might become insecure, awkward and resentful, but Edmund was not any child. He had already developed what is a common trait among those who go on to be serial killers: an appetite for cruelty to animals. When he was ten, he buried a cat alive, then disinterred it, cut off its head and mounted it on a spike. At the age of 13, he tortured and killed another cat when it appeared to favour his sister over him. Even when animals weren't the object of his cruelty, Kemper's childhood games were markedly morbid. Still under the age of ten, he would stalk his teacher's house armed with a bayonet, play at being executed by poison gas or electrocution and dismember his sister's dolls.

On 27 August 1964 at the age of 15, Kemper grew tired of arguing with his grandmother at the kitchen table. He stood, picked up a hunting rifle and fatally shot Maude Kemper once in the head and twice in the back, before stabbing her lifeless body. To avoid an awkward encounter with his grandfather, Emil Kemper Sr, Edmund took the rifle outside and shot the old man dead as he arrived home with the groceries. He then calmly rang his mother and asked for her advice.

Edmund did as he was told: he rang the local police and calmly waited to be arrested. A court found Kemper's crimes beyond comprehension and he was diagnosed with paranoid schizophrenia and detained at Atascadero State Hospital. That facility's psychiatrists disagreed with their court-appointed colleagues; as Kemper was not affected by delusions, hallucinations and chaotic thought, he could not be considered schizophrenic. He was re-diagnosed with "passive-aggressive personality disorder", a defunct clinical term associated with abusive or dysfunctional parenting and consequent repressed anger.

Kemper scored 145 on an IQ test and he demonstrated intelligence in more ways than one. As a model prisoner at Atascadero, he was allowed to help the staff by administering psychiatric tests to sex offenders. Later in life, he would admit that he learned much from this work, not least how to manipulate tests and, by extension, the psychiatrists testing him. This may explain why Kemper was released on parole on his twenty-first birthday in December 1969, and why in November 1972, while he was active as a serial killer, he was considered rehabilitated and his juvenile record was expunged. He had learned to game the system so artfully that, even as he hit his peak as a killer and necrophiliac, he was considered by probation psychiatrists to be no danger to himself or anyone else.

After his release, Kemper lived with his mother, Clarnell, in Aptos in Santa Cruz County, California. Their relationship remained volatile and neighbours became familiar with loud arguments. Kemper studied at community college in compliance with his parole and took a variety of menial jobs, eventually securing employment with the state highways agency and earning enough to get away from Clarnell and move to Alameda.

Kemper's association with California's highways was to prove fateful. After being injured in a road accident, he received compensation that enabled him to buy a Ford Galaxie and begin travelling independently. On his travels, the predator within began to notice the number of young female hitchhikers on California's highways. Kemper dipped his toe in murderous waters gently at first; he picked up an estimated 150 young women on the highway and dropped them off again without incident, even though he had the tools of murder, abduction and dismemberment in the trunk. Time passed and Kemper could no longer resist his lustful, murderous urges, which he nicknamed his little zapples.

In May 1972, Kemper began his final sequence of killings. He and his psychiatrists would later agree that the young women he killed were proxies for his mother, and Kemper claimed that he would seek out victims immediately after arguments with Clarnell. On 7 May, Kemper picked up two hitchhikers in Berkeley, Mary Pesce and Anita Luchessa, both 18-year-old students. He drove them to a secluded woodland spot that he'd scouted out during his day job, handcuffed Mary and locked Anita in the trunk. He later said that he'd chosen the young women because they seemed "of a better class", adding that he'd apologized for accidentally brushing one of Mary's breasts minutes before he murdered her. Both women were stabbed and strangled to death and their bodies transported to Kemper's home.

En route, Kemper was stopped by a police officer, who inspected the Ford Galaxie and brought its driver to book over a broken tail light while remaining oblivious of the two murdered women only inches away. Undaunted, Kemper continued, brought the bodies into his apartment, photographed them, sexually violated them and dismembered them. He later disposed of most of the body parts near Loma Prieta mountain, then violated the heads again before dropping them into a ravine. Mary's skull was eventually found, but no other trace of either woman was recovered.

On 14 September 1972, Kemper offered a lift to 15-year-old Aiko Koo, a dance student who had missed her last bus. Kemper drove her to a secluded spot and threatened her with a firearm before somehow leaving it inside the Ford Galaxie while locking himself out. Koo was induced to let Kemper back in, where he choked her until she passed out before raping and killing her. He then found a nearby bar, where he enjoyed a celebratory drink or two, then brazenly opened the trunk of his car in the bar's car park to admire his handiwork. As with his previous victims, Kemper violated Aiko's remains in his apartment, then dismembered and disposed of them.

No trace of the young woman was ever found.

By 7 January 1973, Kemper had moved back in with Clarnell. On this night, he picked up 18-year-old Cynthia Schall and shot her dead. He hid Cynthia's body in his mother's house overnight; when Clarnell left for work the next day, Kemper violated and dismembered the body, retaining the head for further abuse over several days. While most of the body parts were discarded in the countryside, Cynthia's head was buried in the garden, looking up at Clarnell's bedroom; it was Kemper's idea of a joke that his mother would finally have someone who looked up to her.

Clarnell unknowingly facilitated the final two coed killings. On 5 February 1973, a flaming row with his mother put Kemper in the mood for killing. The authorities were becoming aware that a serial killer was preying on hitchhikers, and local students were advised to accept lifts only from cars bearing university stickers. Clarnell worked at the University of California Santa Cruz (UCSC), so Kemper was able to obtain his own UCSC car sticker through her. He picked up 23-year-old Rosalind Thorpe and 20-year-old Alice Liu on the UCSC campus, drove a short way, then stopped and shot them both in the head. He took their remains back to Clarnell's house and treated them in his usual abhorrent manner before disposing of them the next day.

Kemper's killing spree was about to reach its nadir. On the evening of 20 April 1973, Clarnell woke her son when she returned noisily from a party. A few innocuous words were exchanged and Kemper bade her goodnight. Once she'd fallen asleep, he entered her room, beat her with a claw hammer, slit her throat with a pocket knife and then degraded her remains with sustained, thoughtful hatred. He cut off her head, placed it on a shelf, screamed and threw darts at it, then debased it in his usual manner. He tried and failed to grind up her tongue and vocal cords in the kitchen waste disposal, then he hid what remained of his mother in a cupboard and went out to a bar.

On his return, Kemper invited Clarnell's best friend, 59-year-old Sara Hallett, to join him for dinner and a movie. Despite the lateness of the hour, she made the fatal mistake of agreeing. She was throttled to death and her remains placed in a cupboard alongside Clarnell's. Kemper then left a brief confessional note for the authorities and fled the scene, driving non-stop to Pueblo, Colorado – a journey of around 2,090 km (1,300 mi) – fuelled by caffeine pills and armed with enough guns and ammunition for a final blaze of glory. After indulging in a dramatic escape, however, Kemper was disappointed to discover that the dots had not been joined and he was not the subject of a multi-state manhunt.

A key aspect of hedonistic killing for Kemper was the thrill of recognition. While he was making his reputation as the Coed Killer, he routinely drank and socialized in a bar named The Jury Room, many of whose patrons were police officers to whom Kemper was a chatty drinking buddy they knew as Big Eddie. Remarkably, Kemper had tried to become a police officer around this time but had been rejected because of his height. To what extent The Jury Room's regulars shared the faltering progress of their investigations with their main suspect is not known, but when Big Eddie called Santa Cruz law enforcement from a payphone in Pueblo, Colorado, to confess to murdering his mother, his barroom buddies assumed he was making an audacious joke. While it seems unlikely that Kemper did any of this for comic effect, deriving pleasure both from killing and from manipulating law enforcement is consistent with his hedonistic pathology.

The penny only dropped when Kemper rang again, spoke to an officer with whom he socialized and disclosed details of the modus operandi and crime scenes that only the killer could know. He was arrested without incident and in May 1973 indicted on eight counts of first-degree murder. His vivid and explicit confessions left his defence team only one option: an insanity plea. This failed to meet the M'Naghten standard, a test for insanity in criminal cases used in the UK and some US states.

For a plea of insanity to pass the M'Naghten test, it must be shown that a defendant's reasoning was so impaired that they could not understand what they were doing or, failing this, that they could not know that it was wrong. A clear-minded, articulate and highly organized killer like Kemper was clearly not insane in the eyes of the law. Nevertheless, he remains in a secure psychiatric facility at the time of writing, his request to be tortured to death having not been honoured.

The M'Naghten rule may come across as counter-intuitive or perverse in its definition of sanity. Then again, the M'Naghten rule treats insanity as a legal term of art; it specifically addresses how states of mind intersect with the concept of intent in criminal law. Typically, a defendant cannot be found guilty of a criminal offence unless it can be proved they intended a given result; an altered state of mind can make that proof of intent a tricky proposition, no matter how appalling the crime. That said, a successful so-called insanity plea is far from being a get-out-of-jail card; it can mean that, instead of receiving a fixed-term sentence, a defendant can be detained indefinitely, subject to the judgement of clinicians rather than courts. To use a British legal phrase, they can be held "at His Majesty's pleasure".

While some serial killers may use physical camouflage or cunning subterfuge, others hide in plain sight. For them, one simple fact of human nature is concealment enough: it is difficult for most people to think the unthinkable or believe the unbelievable. Kemper's reign of terror might have ended sooner, and a clearer trail emerged for detectives to follow, had his murders not overlapped with the chaotic killings of Herbert Mullin (see Chapter One). Still, how must the police officers who shared drinks and stories with the supposedly harmless lunkhead, Big Eddie Kemper, have felt when they learned the truth?

FRED AND ROSE WEST: HOUSE OF HORRORS

Between 1967 and 1987, Fred West murdered at least 12 young women in South West England. His wife, Rose West, was jointly concerned in nine of these murders between 1973 and 1987, and also murdered her young stepdaughter in 1971. Many of the killings, together with inconceivable extremities of physical and psychological torture, occurred at the Wests' home, 25 Cromwell Street, Gloucester. This house has since been demolished and its remains ground down and paved over by the local authority. The city needed to forget and ghoulish souvenir hunters needed to be discouraged.

A note of caution is offered at this point. Even given by the diabolical standards of the serial killers with whom the reader has become acquainted thus far, the Wests retain the capacity to shock. It may be simplistic and clichéd to use the term "pure evil" but it is hard to avoid it in this case. The Wests were hedonistic killers who tortured and killed casually, gleefully and without compunction. Helplessness and vulnerability merely added spice to their killings, and they did not draw the line at their own children. For decades, they floated freely in a moral vacuum of their own making.

Fred West was born to a farming family in rural Herefordshire in September 1941, one of six siblings. He was strictly and physically disciplined by his father and doted upon by his mother. He grew up with hard toil and would take a strong work ethic into adult life. He also grew up with an insular outlook and a penchant for petty theft; the family and the home were all that mattered, and the outside world was just a resource to be exploited. West would later claim that his home life in childhood had featured a range of sexual abuse including incest and bestiality. While one of his siblings, Doug West, disputes this, it is the case that West was quite comfortable with incest among other transgressions.

West was also aggressively and unnervingly persistent in his sexual advances towards girls, whoever and wherever they were, seeing them as sources of gratification to be used and discarded. In June 1961, 13-year-old Kitty West told her mother that her then 19-year-old brother Fred had been raping her for months and she was pregnant. West was arrested and in a police interview gave an insight into his warped view of sexuality: he saw no reason to deny that he'd been sexually active with underage girls for years because it was, from his very particular perspective, healthy and normal. Although he was tried before local magistrates, the case against him collapsed when his indulgent mother offered to speak for him and Kitty declined to testify. This scenario would repeat itself, not coincidentally.

In November 1962, Fred West married Rena Costello and moved to her home town in Lanarkshire, Scotland, where he worked as an ice-cream-van driver. It was in this capacity that he killed for what might have been the first time, albeit accidentally; in November 1965, West ran over a small child in his van but a police investigation cleared him of any culpability. West also sank into a pattern that would become lethally familiar; family life was defined by various forms of physical and sexual abuse, violent misogyny and sexual incontinence.

West's own daughter with Costello, Anna Marie, and Rena's child by a previous relationship, Charmaine, were held in an improvised cage while he was in the house. West had numerous affairs and Costello retaliated in kind. When West discovered her in a clinch with her lover, John McLachlan, he instinctively struck Rena. A brief fracas ensued between the two men but West became submissive when it was clear that McLachlan was not intimidated. McLachlan allegedly beat West several times in retaliation for his assaulting Costello, and later offered the opinion that, while Fred West seized upon any opportunity to assault women, he had no appetite for attacking men.

By February 1966, Fred West, fearing local reprisals for the ice-cream-van incident, had moved to Gloucester with his dysfunctional family: Rena Costello, their nanny Isa McNeill, a family friend Anne McFall and the children Anna Marie and Charmaine. This toxic ménage shared West's caravan and it became a cramped vision of Hell. He terrorized the three women with threatened and actual violence, and physically and sexually abused Charmaine. Rena was encouraged to become a street sex worker to top up West's income as a lorry driver for an abattoir.

For several years, this diabolical soap opera unravelled. Costello moved back and forth to Scotland, intermittently leaving the children. The local police adjudicated on various domestic disturbances and accusations of theft. McFall hitched her wagon to West and tried to persuade him to marry her and divorce Costello. In July 1967, McFall vanished; she was 18 years old and eight months pregnant with West's child. She was so alone in the world, but for the monster to whom she'd been shackled, that nobody ever reported her missing. In June 1994, McFall's dismembered remains would be found on farmland near Fred's childhood home in Herefordshire, her wrists still bound together.

Rose West (née Letts) met Fred in 1969 when she was 15 and he 27. She was born in the Devon market town of Northam in 1953, one of seven siblings. Her family life was blighted by poverty, abuse and mental illness: her mother received electroconvulsive therapy for depression, and her father was a sexually and physically abusive schizophrenic. Rose's own sexuality was dysfunctional and cruel, possibly an enactment or normalization of the abuse she'd suffered. By the age of 13, she was sexually abusing her two younger brothers, both beneath the age of ten.

Fred and Rose met at a bus stop in Cheltenham. He was unkempt and malodorous and she found him repellent, but he persisted in his pursuit of her to the point where she agreed to date him. Theirs would be a match made in Hell: she was frank about her appetite for transgressive sex and he about his wish for more children. They would, over time, discover that they had much else in common. After Anne McFall's disappearance and the breakdown of Fred's relationship with Rena Costello, Charmaine and Anna Marie were briefly taken into care. Unfortunately for them, this was only temporary and they were returned to Hell with Rose as the chief tormentor.

Dysfunctional as Rose's parents were, they were still horrified by her relationship with Fred. Social services were obliged to intervene due to her being underage and pregnant with his child, and, while Fred did serve several prison sentences between 1969 and 1971, these were for petty theft and unpaid fines and not for any sexual offences. Rose remained devoted to Fred West and by 1971, at the age of 17, she was stepmother to Charmaine and Anna Marie, and new mother to her own baby, Heather Ann.

It seemed that, when it came to sustained, considered cruelty, Fred had nothing to teach Rose. While they lived in a basement apartment at Midland Road, Gloucester, Anna Marie and Charmaine developed different responses to abuse. While Anna Marie gave Rose what she wanted in the form of tears, pleas and a submissive posture, Charmaine would remain dry-eyed and defiant under the blows. Enhanced punishment for Charmaine might entail being beaten with a wooden spoon while naked, bound and gagged.

Fred and Rose were uncannily well matched. Calculating the odds against two such very particular personality types meeting and hitting it off would be an intriguing project for a statistically adept criminologist or psychologist. That aside, Fred and Rose would inspire new depths of cruelty in one another, enacting their impulses often but not always in concert. Indeed, Rose committed her first murder on her own initiative. In June 1971, shortly before Fred's release from prison, a friend of Charmaine's called for her only to be told she'd gone to stay with her mother. Anna Marie was later and repeatedly taunted with the same gloating lie. When Fred got home, he proved himself the right man for Rose: he took Charmaine's body from where Rose had hidden it – in the coal cellar of their ground-floor apartment – and buried it in the rear garden. It may be that yet another sadistic beating had robbed this brave, doomed girl of her life.

Rena Costello, frantic about the welfare of her children, was next to place her head in the lion's jaws. She is known to have travelled to Gloucester from Scotland in August 1971 to make enquiries and confront Fred. She confided her plans in her sister-in-law and was never seen alive again. Fred sexually abused her with a metal tube, then throttled the life out of her in the narrow confines of an old Ford Popular. Her remains were split among numerous plastic bags and buried near Fred's childhood home in Herefordshire.

In early 1972, Fred and Rose married and moved into 25 Cromwell Street, Gloucester. In June, Rose gave birth to their second daughter, Mae June. Cromwell Street is made up of three-storey Victorian terraces built in the 1850s for well-to-do residents of this prosperous cathedral city. When the Wests purchased number 25, they could only afford to do so by subletting several upper-storey rooms. While Cromwell Street's houses may have originally been intended for a burgeoning Victorian middle class and their servants, rapid social change over generations meant that handsome multistorey Victorian terraces could house a more varied demographic.

Terraced dwellings were once a novel concept and were initially needed to house increasing numbers of rural workers drawn into towns and cities by the Industrial Revolution. Today, such houses can provide roomy single dwellings for wealthy urbanites or can be ruthlessly subdivided and rented out for a high profit margin to those living below the poverty threshold in urban spaces. It is noteworthy that a house of this era usually featured a cellar below street level intended for the storage of coal and perishable goods; coal was delivered in such large quantities that merchants would deliver it directly into the cellar via a hatch or chute. Those cellars were cold, damp and cramped by design and were never intended for human habitation. They were, however, ideal for other activities.

Within months of Mae June's arrival, Fred and Rose began to search for new vices. She used one of their bedsit rooms to earn from sex work and also engaged in casual sex with both male and female lodgers, sometimes involving Fred too. Rose and Fred fed each other's cruelty, and they developed a taste for inflicting sexual sadism and dominance on women. Practices ranged from suffocation to penetration with outsize objects and the couple amassed a collection of bondage equipment and extreme pornography. So normal did the abnormal become that Rose's father, Bill Letts, became one of her clients, paying to engage in paternal incest. Rose would ultimately give birth to eight children, an unknown number of whom were the result of sex work and worse.

Breaking profound moral taboos became normalized for the Wests. Evil was perpetrated for convenience and ephemeral thrills. The various children cursed to be born into their world became prisoners, enslaved people, punchbags and worse. Their abuse was methodical; however, Rose ensured that their injuries didn't extend to faces, hands or any other areas that might be visible at school. Remarkably, the West children were hospitalized 31 times over 20 years with no involvement from social services. The abuse went beyond beatings: from the age of eight, Anna Marie was raped by Fred with the enthusiastic involvement of Rose, who told the child it was a normal aspect of family life.

In December 1972, Fred decided to acquaint Rose with the excitement of abduction and murder. They had hired 17-year-old Caroline Owens as a nanny but she had been disturbed by the couple's aggressive sexual advances and quit. They found her hitchhiking on the A40 road, enticed her into their car with fulsome apologies, sexually assaulted her, punched her unconscious, tied her up and transported her to the cellar of 25 Cromwell Street. In the coal cellar, she was bound, gagged, partially smothered, subjected to sadistic sex games amounting to torture and threatened with murder and gang rape for screaming loudly enough to prompt awkward questions from the West children.

Caroline Owens survived but another opportunity to stop the Wests was lost. In a surreal segue, Fred switched from threatening death and bragging about his killings to asking Caroline if she fancied resuming her job as nanny. A survival instinct prompted her to agree and she went through the motions of performing housework. She was later taken by Rose to a launderette and took the chance to flee, finding her way home, where she eventually confided in her mother, who informed the police. The Wests were arrested, charged with various counts of assault and rape and placed before local magistrates in January 1973. So horrified was Caroline, however, that she couldn't face her assailants in court, and the Wests walked free having pleaded guilty to a few minor offences.

The Wests had thoroughly enjoyed their abuse of Caroline Owens and may have been emboldened by the seeming impotence of the justice system. Their first joint murder – as far as is known – occurred in April 1973. An acquaintance of a lodger, 19-year-old Lynda Gough, moved into 25 Cromwell Street and promptly disappeared. Her mother, who bravely confronted the Wests and found Rose wearing her daughter's clothes, was told by the Wests that Lynda had struck one of their children and been asked to leave. The reality was unimaginably grim and can only be inferred from forensic discoveries made decades too late.

The Wests learned from their experience with Caroline Owens and honed their craft. Lynda Gough's jaw was taped shut with an abundance of DIY and surgical tape and tubes inserted into her nostrils; she could thus be kept alive but could not audibly scream for help. She had been suspended by the wrists from holes drilled into the cellar's ceiling beams. She and other victims may also have been strangled or suffocated by similar means. With each new victim, the abuse became more sustained and inventive as the Wests sought new thrills.

Between November 1973 and April 1975, four young women and two children would be tortured to death in this dank space. They were Lynda Gough, 19, Carol Cooper, 15, Lucy Partington, 21, Thérèse Siegenthaler, 21, Shirley Hubbard, 15, and Juanita Mott, 18. Most were abducted from public places and had no prior acquaintance with the Wests. Five would be buried in the dirt of the floor of the cellar where they had been tormented, murdered and dismembered. After disposing of Juanita Mott, Fred West concreted over the cellar floor and turned it into accommodation for his growing brood.

In May 1978, 18-year-old Shirley Robinson disappeared from 25 Cromwell Street while eight months pregnant with Fred's child. It is likely that the murder of her and her unborn child was a matter of convenience for Fred, echoing the fate of Anne McFall. The Wests' final joint sexual murder, at least as far as is known, occurred in August 1979. Alison Chambers was a troubled 16-year-old who had absconded from care to become the Wests' nanny. The dismembered remains of Shirley and Alison would later be found in the back garden of 25 Cromwell Street but they wouldn't be the only ones.

Still the horror rolled on, seemingly endless. In 1979, Anna Marie West ran away from home and Fred turned his sexual attentions to Heather and Mae. These poor, brave girls devised survival strategies: they would allow a degree of sexual interference with humorous acceptance to placate Fred, make sure they were never showering or unclothed when he was in the house and try to remain in each other's company. Stephen West had been warned he'd have to have sex with his mother, Rose, by the age of 17, but fortunately for him he was evicted when he turned 16.

Remarkably, Heather West was doing well at school, but teachers became concerned. There were physical signs of abuse and Rose's sexual adventures with paying clients and casual lovers had filtered into the student rumour mill. Tragically, this led not to intervention from the authorities but to a brutal reckoning at home. Heather was badgered into confirming the rumours by friends, and her words found their way back to Fred, who bided his time.

In June 1987, a year after leaving school, Heather sought any escape route she could find and was heartbroken when she was turned down for a residential job at a holiday camp 209 km (130 mi) away in Torquay, Devon. Her siblings heard her sobbing all through the night; when they bade her farewell on their way to school the next morning, they were seeing her for the last time. Fred and Rose would taunt the rest of their children with one poor lie after another: Heather had got the Torquay job after all, she'd had a row and run away *and* she was in trouble over credit-card fraud. Unable to help himself, Fred also threatened the children with a smile on his face that they would end up under the patio like Heather if they didn't behave. Heather had been sexually assaulted, murdered, dismembered and buried in the back garden by her parents.

The unravelling began in 1992. Fred raped, sodomized and partially choked 13-year-old Louise West. She broke down and told a friend; that friend told a parent, who told the police. All the children at 25 Cromwell Street were removed and placed into care, and the marks on their bodies told an unignorable story. The investigation into sexual abuse ended in an agonizing acquittal for the Wests when neither Louise nor Anna Marie would testify. The children remained in foster care, however, and it was beginning to dawn on the police that Heather and other women and children associated with the Wests remained missing and wholly unaccounted for. Detective Constable Hazel Savage would later be honoured for her tenacity in uncovering their fate. In February 1994, local magistrates granted police permission to search 25 Cromwell Street for Heather West's remains. Fred's joke about burying his daughter under the patio would come to look like hubris.

Even before the excavations could begin in earnest, Fred confessed to killing Heather, claiming he had done so in a fit of rage rather than with premeditation. As the excavation proceeded slowly and methodically, and more and more bodies emerged from that wretched hellscape, Fred confessed his guilt incrementally while denying Rose's involvement.

An abiding memory of that winter for both the citizens of Gloucester and crime reporters across the world is the sight of police officers in blue boiler suits with spades and excavators gouging away the earth behind a humdrum terraced house; later, tents and screens would be erected to deter hardcore voyeurs and paparazzi.

Both Fred and Rose West were charged with multiple murders. Rose has always maintained her innocence, regardless of which she was convicted of ten counts of murder in November 1995 and sentenced to life with no chance of parole. Fred cheated justice, hanging himself with an improvised ligature at HMP Birmingham in January 1995.

It is probable that between them, the Wests murdered numerous other young women and children, who will remain classified as missing persons indefinitely. Fred West claimed to have murdered up to 30 individuals in total, leaving 18 unaccounted for. While he was eventually forthcoming about the murders with which he was charged, he was cryptic about other possibilities. One such is that he killed several young women in Glasgow during the 1960s; the allotment that Fred rented back then, and in which he dug so energetically while never producing any vegetables, now lies deep under the concrete foundations of the M8 motorway.

That there is no such thing as normal in family life is a tired old aphorism, but it is a bleak summary of the underlying pathologies of Fred and Rose West. In their backgrounds, grotesquely abnormal expressions of sexuality and familial relationships were normalized to the point of banality by repetition. A distinctive feature of all the human remains exhumed in 1994 was that small bones, sometimes from the hands and feet, were missing. It is thought that the Wests liked to keep souvenirs. Perhaps robbing their victims of their dignity, their hope and their lives wasn't quite cruel enough to thrill them. Fred never told the police where those bones lie now, and Rose never will.

KENNETH BIANCHI: THE CLEVER MALINGERER

Between October 1977 and January 1979, Kenneth Bianchi murdered 12 young women and children. Bianchi killed ten of his victims in Los Angeles, USA, in partnership with his cousin, Angelo Buono, earning the nickname the Hillside Strangler. He murdered his final two victims solo in Washington State.

Kenneth Bianchi is the archetype of the hedonistic serial killer. What makes his story so profoundly chilling is the extent to which he apparently savoured every part of the process of hunting, torturing, raping and killing with discernment and calculation. Even after his arrest, he found ways to sustain his enjoyment by making fools of court-appointed psychiatrists, deploying wit, guile and academic acumen. His police mugshot is particularly striking: whereas police pictures of serial killers often show vivid emotions ranging from confusion to defiance to euphoria, Bianchi is self-contained and content with his own wisdom, smiling inscrutably to himself like a moustached Mona Lisa.

Bianchi had an unhappy start in life. He was born in Rochester, New York, in May 1951 to a teenage sex worker. He was adopted soon after by Nicholas Bianchi and Frances Scioliono-Bianchi and brought up as their only child. While he is believed to have had a stable home background, Kenneth was nonetheless a troubled and troubling child. He lied inventively and incessantly, endured petit mal seizures and wetted the bed, all of which resulted in visits to clinicians with consequent self-consciousness verging on humiliation.

Bianchi was also remarkably intelligent, scoring 116 in an IQ test at the age of 11. Despite this, he was an underachiever at school, a situation that wasn't improved by his adoptive mother frequently keeping him at home after his adoptive father died. He did, however, graduate from high school and marry his sweetheart, Brenda Beck, in 1970, although she left him for unknown reasons eight months later.

Bianchi would develop and retain an interest in becoming a police officer, although this would never be fulfilled. He also took a strong interest in psychology both generally and specifically as it applied to law enforcement. While both disciplines would continue to fascinate him, he seemingly lacked the application to fulfil his ambitions, dropping out of a college course combining police science and psychology after one term and finding work instead as a security guard in a jewellery shop. In this role, he began to demonstrate a starkly transactional and amoral approach to some of his needs: he cheerfully betrayed his employer's trust by stealing jewellery that he then used to pay for sex from sex workers or to buy the loyalty of girlfriends. He also tried and failed to join his local sheriff's department.

At the heart of Bianchi's offending is a clear contempt for women. In 1976, he moved to Los Angeles and got acquainted with his adoptive cousin, Angelo Buono, whose greatest pleasure in life was dominating and subordinating women. A pair of ruthless, enterprising misogynists, they kindled one another's enthusiasms, first becoming pimps, exploiting vulnerable women for money. They then took the next step and became recreational murderers of women.

On 17 October 1977, 19-year-old Yolanda Washington was found close to the highway off Forest Lawn Drive in Los Angeles. She had been bound by the neck, arms and legs, raped, beaten and throttled, then left in a sexually degrading posture in full public view so that a final misogynistic insult could be added to terminal injury. It would later emerge that Bianchi and Buono had persuaded Yolanda into their car by pretending to be plain-clothes police officers.

Bianchi and Buono would continue to follow this pattern into early 1978, with occasional variations. While abduction, sexual abuse, strangulation and post-mortem humiliation were always indulged in, other techniques were tried. On 20 November 1977, for example, 20-year-old Kristina Weckler was tortured by being injected with window-cleaning fluid before being asphyxiated with oven gas. On 28 November 1977, 18-year-old Lauren Wagner was handcuffed and burned with electricity. The pair didn't restrict themselves to adults: on 13 November 1977, they abducted 12-year-old Dolores Cepeda and 14-year-old Sonja Johnson and inflicted their usual modus operandi on both girls.

Bianchi and Buono's partnership came to an end in February 1978 when Bianchi disclosed that, between murders, he'd applied to join the Los Angeles Police Department and had been on ride-alongs with the very police officers hunting them. While Bianchi was clearly pleased with himself, Buono was less impressed and threatened to kill his partner in crime if he didn't leave town.

There appears to have been a hiatus of almost a year in Bianchi's killing career, during which time he relocated to Washington State. On 11 January 1979, Bianchi was employed as a security guard at a house in Bellingham. He exploited his status to lure two Western Washington University students into the house. Karen Mandic, 22, and Diane Wilder, 27, were both strangled to death in a chaotic fashion and Bianchi was arrested on 12 January. The trail of evidence he'd left behind him, not least the fact that his identification and job status linked him to the crime scene, hinted strongly at the organizational role Buono had played in the pair's LA murders.

Bianchi offered a plea of not guilty by reason of insanity and the psychiatric profession joined the fray. He managed to convince several experts that "Steven Walker", an uncontrollable alter ago, had committed the crimes with Bianchi as a helpless passenger. If this claim held, then Bianchi's plea might succeed and, worse, his evidence could not be used against Buono. Psychologist Martin Orne was asked to consult and made some striking discoveries.

Orne pointed out that multiple personality disorder (MPD) usually involved a minimum of three alter egos; Bianchi immediately created "Billy", an imaginary lawyer with whom he shook hands, causing confusion when his real lawyer entered. Orne noted that while tactile hallucinations were theorized, he had never seen a real one. Investigators discovered that not only did Bianchi possess a small, well-thumbed library of contemporary psychology texts, but he also had once attempted to steal the identity and credentials of a bona fide psychology student named Steven Walker.

Orne concluded that Bianchi was "a clever malingerer" and that while he had antisocial personality disorder with sexual sadism, he was not delusional for the purposes of criminal law. Bianchi changed his approach and agreed to testify against Buono in exchange for a reduced sentence. Buono was arrested for the Los Angeles murders and tried, largely on the basis of Bianchi's confessions. The fact that Bianchi had given his testimony in a spirit of self-interest and mischief-making made his evidence contentious. While Buono was eventually convicted, his murder trial was the longest in US history, taking a full two years. As of 2024, both men remain incarcerated.

A possibility remains that Bianchi was responsible for the still-unsolved "Alphabet" murders of three children in Rochester, New York, between 1971 and 1973. While he worked nearby at the time and fitted the profile, he denies any involvement and sufficient proof to prosecute any suspect is unlikely to emerge.

The files of police departments all over the world bear the names of legions of missing people, many of whom will never be found. The lists of murders ascribed to and proven against history's most egregious serial killers are often and inevitably incomplete. While reasons for rationing the truth vary from killer to killer, in the case of Bianchi it is likely that he would reveal the truth, and grant peace to traumatized families, only if it benefited and entertained him to do so. This is wholly consistent with the modus operandi of a hedonistic serial killer: Bianchi killed to satisfy his personal desires and was indifferent to the suffering of others unless it could offer him fresh thrills.

RODNEY ALCALA: BACHELOR NUMBER ONE

Between 1968 and 1979, Rodney Alcala is known to have killed at least eight women and children in the US states of California, New York and Wyoming. So prolific a killer was Alcala that the real number of victims could be up to 130. In the decades that have passed since his arrest and conviction, police inquiries inspired by Alcala's photograph collection have opened a Pandora's box of horror and loss.

While many infamous serial killers are hedonistic, killing primarily for personal gratification, few have enjoyed public attention quite as much as Alcala. He is perhaps most notorious for fitting in an appearance on a TV dating show while he was actively hunting and killing young women. While at first glance it might seem unwise for a serial killer to attract so much public attention, it is in fact wholly consistent with a particular kind of pathology.

Rodney James Alcala was born Rodrigo Jacques Alcala in San Antonio, Texas, in 1943. Dislocation and abandonment featured in his childhood, his father moving the family to Mexico when Alcala was eight, then abandoning them. A few years later, the single-parent family moved to Los Angeles, where Alcala would graduate from high school, apparently a popular, intelligent and settled boy.

Armies of every nationality look for the ideal balance of aggression and self-discipline in their recruits. When Alcala joined the US Army in 1961 at the age of 17, he was wholly unfit for purpose, bringing a warped form of aggression impervious to discipline. Insubordination was just the beginning of his dire military record, which would escalate to assaults on young women and a dishonourable discharge following a diagnosis of antisocial personality disorder by an army psychiatrist, who also noted an IQ score of 135.

Such a setback might have condemned a lesser serial killer to a life of dead-end jobs and petty acquisitive crime, but Alcala had a talent for bouncing back from adversity and making the most of his dark good looks, his intelligence and his confidence. After leaving the US Army, he graduated from college and studied film-making in New York under controversial movie director Roman Polanski.

Yet Alcala would always put his extracurricular activities above conventional career goals. In September 1968, a vigilant passerby saw eight-year-old Tali Shapiro being lured into Alcala's LA apartment, smelled a rat and called the police. When officers entered, they found Tali unconscious and bloody, having been raped and beaten comatose with a metal bar. Alcala had fled and would remain a wanted fugitive until 1971.

Alcala relocated to New York and took the name John Berger. In June 1971, he strangled 23-year-old flight attendant Cornelia Crilley to death in her Manhattan apartment after she'd accepted his help to move furniture. This crime would remain unsolved until 2011. In August 1971, guests at a New Hampshire arts camp recognized a face in an FBI wanted poster; the camp's children's counsellor, Mr Berger, was identified as Alcala, arrested and extradited to California.

His luck remained diabolically good, however; not only did the authorities remain ignorant of his murder of Cornelia Crilley – and potentially others still unknown – but Tali Shapiro's family had left the USA and would not allow their traumatized daughter to return to testify. Shapiro served a shorter sentence on a lesser offence and regained his liberty in 1974. He repeated this feat again almost immediately: he abducted and sexually assaulted a 13-year-old girl, served only two years and was free yet again in 1977. When he killed repeatedly in the late 1970s, and when he enjoyed his 15 minutes of fame on a TV dating show, he did so as a registered sex offender.

After his release in 1977, Alcala promptly resumed his killing. Ellen Hover, 23-year-old god-daughter of showbusiness royalty Dean Martin and Sammy Davis Jr, went missing in July having noted an appointment with "John Berger" in her diary. This name led the FBI to Alcala, but he admitted nothing of worth and could not be charged as there was no proof of murder. Ellen's body would later be discovered under rocks near the Rockefeller Estate in upstate New York. At least one would-be model reported that Alcala, a.k.a. Berger, had photographed her at this location.

Photography would be a key feature of Alcala's modus operandi in an unknowable number of murders. He persuaded many young men and women that he was a professional photographer building a portfolio, and many agreed to help by joining him on shoots in picturesque and secluded locations. For aspiring models, a free photo shoot is a boon, and some were lucky enough to get just that. Others got a wholly different experience.

Alcala committed the majority of his known killings between November 1977 and June 1979. Jill Barcomb, 18, was found dead near Mulholland Drive on 9 November 1977 having been sexually assaulted, beaten and throttled to death. Georgia Wixted, 27, was sexually assaulted, savagely beaten to death and intimately mutilated in her Malibu apartment on 16 December 1977. Charlotte Lamb, 31, was sexually assaulted and throttled with a shoelace in the laundry room of her El Segundo apartment block on 24 June 1978.

On 14 February 1979, Alcala used a bit more of his diabolical luck. Monique Hoyt, 15, was picked up by Alcala while hitchhiking in Riverside County, California. He subjected her to rape in multiple locations, including his home and remote areas of Joshua Tree, photographing some of his exploits. Despite the fact that she'd been beaten unconscious with a rock, Monique escaped when Alcala entered a gas station and she lived to tell the tale. He was arrested, then, unbelievably, released again when his mother posted bail for him.

Thanks to the largesse of Alcala's mother, at least two more people would die terrifying deaths. On 13 June 1979, Jill Parenteau, 21, was found dead in her Burbank apartment having been sexually assaulted, beaten and throttled. Later that week, on 20 June 1979, Robin Samsoe, 12, vanished after setting off on a bicycle for her ballet class in Huntington Beach. She was raped, beaten and stabbed to death and her remains dumped in the San Gabriel Mountains.

For all his intelligence, confidence and premeditation, Alcala was an untidy killer. He was, to take one example, seen and later identified by potential victims close to the scene of Robin Samsoe's disappearance. He left his blood at Jill Parenteau's apartment having cut himself while breaking in, and intimate trace evidence at several other crime scenes that would lead to charges and convictions when DNA analysis came of age. The final such instance came about in 2016 when Alcala was charged with the murder of Christine Thornton, missing since June 1977 and whose remains were found alongside a lonely, wind-scoured highway in Sweetwater County, Wyoming, in 1982. She had been six months pregnant when she died, and her picture was in Alcala's portfolio.

Alcala was arrested for the final time in July 1979, given no chance of bail, found guilty of Robin Samsoe's murder and sentenced to death. The story of Alcala's lengthy and inventive appeals process, and the numerous subsequent charges and convictions laid at his door, is a long one; suffice it to say that he would never again be free to kill. Alcala was undoubtedly afflicted by antisocial behaviour disorder, which is associated with perceived abandonment or rejection in childhood and can lead to an inability to trust and a reliance on – and an enjoyment of – deception and manipulation. This meant that being seen as normal and hiding in plain sight delivered an intoxicating thrill.

It is noteworthy that hedonistic serial killers can be highly creative in extracting thrills both from stalking and killing their victims, and from playing cat and mouse with both law enforcement and the mass media. Appearing as a safe, eligible, harmless potential boyfriend for a girl next door on TV game show *The Dating Game* in 1978 must have polished Alcala's ego to a high sheen. "We're going to have a great time together, Cheryl," said Alcala during the show, adding, "the best time is at night... night-time's when it really gets good." Clips of Alcala's TV appearance are still viewable on YouTube and other websites, and the incident inspired the 2023 Netflix crime thriller *Woman of the Hour*.

The plans Alcala had for his date with Cheryl are not known, although subverting the whole medium with a disappearance and a murder must have crossed his mind. Luckily for Cheryl Bradshaw, however, she followed her instincts. As reported in *The Guardian* in the UK and other media, she told the show's producers: "I can't go out with this guy. There's [sic] weird vibes... coming off him. He's very strange. I am not comfortable." It is noteworthy that, at that time, contestants on such shows weren't background-checked; Alcala already had a criminal record for sexual assault and violence against a minor.

There but for the grace of God went Cheryl Bradshaw. Chilling as her brush with evil was, contemplating Alcala's trove of photographs opens up a yawning gulf of misery and horror. In 2010, police departments in both New York and California shared 120 photographs with the general public. These images were drawn from Alcala's collection and may have represented both souvenirs and trophies to him. The police declined to share a further 900 images, because they featured intimate degradation. While a number of women fortunate enough to have survived would identify themselves, half a dozen families picked out family members who had been reported missing and never located.

Most of the pictures remain publicly available and they are likely to depict a significant number of cold-case victims. In July 2021, after decades of gratifyingly high-profile legal shenanigans, Rodney Alcala cheated the executioner by dying of a heart attack. Any slender chance of closure for the families of so many missing women and children may have died with him.

GORDON CUMMINS: THE BLACKOUT RIPPER

Between 1888 and 1891, an unidentified serial killer known as Jack the Ripper murdered and mutilated five women in the dark, foggy slums of Victorian London. The term "Ripper" has been applied to other serial killers infamous for targeting and mutilating women, most famously Peter Sutcliffe. There is, however, another British killer who had a better claim to the name Ripper, for he too stalked coal-black, smoke-stained London streets in pursuit of his victims and ripped at their mortal remains with diabolical spite.

Gordon Cummins murdered at least four women and attempted to murder two others in London in February 1942. The Second World War was raging and gave Cummins both opportunity and camouflage. He is more popularly known as the Blackout Ripper because he took advantage of the blackout, an enforced embargo on artificial lighting intended to make it more difficult for the Luftwaffe to find and bomb British cities. During the wartime blackout, citizens of combatant nations had to adapt to levels of darkness not experienced since before the advent of widespread street and domestic lighting generations earlier.

Gordon Cummins was born in New Earswick, North Yorkshire, England, in 1914. His father ran a school for errant youths and his mother was a stay-at-home parent, but Cummins may not have spent much of his childhood at home, as he was sent to Llandovery in Wales to be privately educated. Whether he endured any formative trauma at home or at school is not known, but his teachers later recalled that he'd focused far more on socializing than on his studies. He abandoned education at the age of 18 and in early adulthood failed to settle, getting sacked from several jobs for poor timekeeping.

Cummins did, however, excel in one self-appointed role, that of ersatz aristocrat. In a manner reminiscent of Percy Toplis – the infamous British rogue, army deserter and murderer active during and shortly after the First World War – Cummins learned that he could live the life of society's upper crust by imitating its accent and manners. It is a distinct possibility that he suffered the kind of antisocial personality disorder that made deception and manipulation sources of power, fascination and fulfilment.

Cummins moved to London in 1934 and became a leather dresser in a clothing factory. He also threw himself wholeheartedly into an alternative life as a gentleman: he perfected the accent and appearance of an upper-class Oxford graduate and insisted on being referred to as the Honourable Gordon Cummins. So equipped, he became a familiar face in fashionable clubs and hotels in London's West End, convincing their regulars and staff that he was the illegitimate son of a peer of the realm. It is noteworthy that he profited from this charade only psychologically; while he no doubt exulted in the thrill of deception, and he bragged about the sexual conquests that flowed from it, he was living far beyond his humble means. Indeed, he had to steal to bankroll his lifestyle and even this wasn't enough. When he was fired from his day job for poor performance, he was forced to reassess.

In 1935, Cummins joined the peacetime Royal Air Force (RAF) as an engineer. This would give him a steady wage with meals and housing; it would also give him new opportunities for betterment, both real and imagined. While it is easy to see Cummins's play-acting as cynically self-interested, the possibility remains that he believed his own lies devoutly and was inspired by a deep-seated sense of need, resentment or entitlement. His fellow RAF engineers found his claims of nobility tedious and objectionable and labelled him "the Duke" and "the Count".

In 1936, Cummins courted and married Marjorie Stevens, who worked for a glamorous West End impresario. When the Second World War broke out, he was still serving in the RAF in a technical trade. While he craved advancement, and aspired to fly the famous British fighter aircraft, the Spitfire, by 1941 he still held the relatively junior, enlisted rank of Leading Aircraftman. To his small credit, there was substance to his ambition; he notched up 1,000 hours of flying time and was accepted for aircrew training in early 1942. To his shame, he couldn't quite keep himself on the right side of the line and was suspected of stealing jewellery from the owner of a social club frequented by the RAF. He was lucky that the police could find no evidence, as in the 1940s even famous, decorated fighter pilots could be drummed out of the service for offences as minor as bouncing cheques.

By early 1942, the frequency of enemy air attacks on the UK had diminished since the Blitz, but the risk remained and so did blackout conditions. Air-Raid Precautions (ARP) wardens were the much-maligned volunteers whose work included making sure that no artificial light was visible outside buildings. They generally succeeded in this, and, according to the Imperial War Museum, by January 1942 an estimated one in five British citizens had sustained injuries attributable to the blackout, many in road accidents. London in the early war years was thus almost completely unlit in the hours of darkness; it also sported the scars of war in the form of buildings blighted or wholly displaced by craters and rubble.

When the air-raid sirens weren't wailing, London's battered streets were thronged by a fascinating cast of characters. Men and – to a lesser but significant extent – women in military uniform, of many trades and nationalities, enjoyed the thrills of the city before they returned to their dangerous postings. Police officers, generally too old for front-line military service, tried to keep the antics of fit young soldiers, sailors and aircrew within acceptable limits. ARP wardens and firefighters were on hand in case of air attack and it paid to know the location of the nearest air-raid shelter. Waiters, bartenders and cooks sustained the revels by hook and by crook despite wartime rationing. Sex workers plied a booming trade among lonely, homesick and lustful young men. When the sun went down, all of these people would lead their brisk and sometimes brief lives in indoor oases of light and laughter divided by expanses of rubble-strewn darkness.

Against this backdrop, Cummins waged his brief, horrific campaign of serial murder. What prompted this sudden, drastic escalation will never be known, because the usual precursor offences either didn't happen or are simply missing from the narrative. On 8 February 1942, Cummins began a period of leave, visited his wife in Southwark, borrowed money from her and headed off to the West End for a supposedly solitary night on the town. A little before midnight, 41-year-old pharmacist Evelyn Hamilton left a café at Marble Arch and set out to walk home in the dark. She was seized by Cummins, fought with him in the shadows and rubble, and was subdued, sexually assaulted, throttled to death and robbed. Her remains were found in an air-raid shelter in Marylebone.

It appears that Cummins remained in London for several days, and he was known to keep temporary lodgings in St John's Wood. On the evening of 9 February 1942 on Shaftesbury Avenue, 34-year-old Evelyn Oatley was seen being propositioned by a man who met Cummins's description. Evelyn worked as both a nightclub hostess and a sex worker in the West End and such frank conversations may not have been unusual for her. Her body was discovered the following morning in her Soho apartment in a condition reminiscent of the Whitechapel murders of the 1880s. She had been beaten and strangled and her throat had been fatally cut. Among other violations, Evelyn's belly, thighs and genitals had then been mutilated in a thorough and leisurely fashion with a safety razor and a tin opener. A set of left-handed fingerprints were recovered from various bloodstained objects.

Cummins seemed set on a killing spree during that dreadful week. His legacy has been muted because it coincided with the endless horror of the Second World War. For similar reasons, and because the British press dutifully observed wartime reporting restrictions in part to protect public morale, his murders received limited contemporary coverage. News did spread, however, particularly among West End hostesses and sex workers, for whom the Blackout Ripper was a greater risk than German bombs.

In the small hours of 11 February 1942, 43-year-old sex worker Margaret Lowe was murdered in her Marylebone apartment. Her remains were discovered by her teenage daughter on 13 February and the horror can barely be imagined. Margaret had been extensively mutilated and various blades and a fire poker protruded from her body. Among other debasements, her viscera and uterus had been raggedly ripped open. More left-handed fingerprints were recovered.

On 12 February 1942, 25-year-old sex worker Catherine Mulcahy had a lucky escape. Having solicited sex from Catherine on Regent Street, Cummins accompanied her to her apartment and tried to throttle her. She fought him off and ran to a neighbour's apartment, only to be followed by a calm Cummins, who apologized, threw money at her and fled, inadvertently leaving behind his RAF webbing belt. Shortly after his attempt on the life of Catherine Mulcahy, Cummins solicited sex from 32-year-old Doris Jouannet and murdered and mutilated her in her Bayswater apartment. She had been throttled with her stockings and the flesh around her belly and genitals had been gashed or hacked away.

Doris Jouannet would be Cummins's final murder victim, but he would make one more reckless attempt. On 13 February 1942, he propositioned and harassed Margaret Heywood in Piccadilly. She repeatedly attempted to put him off and take her leave of him but he wouldn't be deterred, grabbed her by the throat and tried to force her into a doorway. As Margaret lost consciousness, a delivery boy heard the commotion in the dark and investigated, saving Margaret's life and prompting Cummins to flee, leaving behind his RAF gas mask and haversack. Cummins had enough acumen to realize that he was leaving a trail of collateral evidence and so, with an alibi in mind, he stole another man's mask and haversack and returned to base.

Local detectives acted commendably quickly. By 11.30 p.m. on 13 February, they had liaised with the RAF Police, who established that the discarded gas mask and haversack had been issued to Cummins and that Cummins had yet to return to base. Cummins was arrested on 14 February 1942 and would protest his innocence all the way to the gallows. By the standards of the day, the forensic and eyewitness evidence against him was strong, and he damned himself by blatantly attempting to falsify records of his movements and by keeping souvenirs from the four murders of February 1942. When he went on trial for his life in April 1942, he affected indifference to the proceedings and made light-hearted banter with his counsel. He also made the mistake of speaking in his own defence, having overestimated his powers of charm and persuasion. The jury took a little over half an hour to find him guilty.

Cummins was hanged in June 1942. Supervising his execution was the famous second-generation hangman, Albert Pierrepoint, at whose hands up to 600 condemned prisoners, including Nazi war criminals, would meet their end. It is commonly believed that Pierrepoint shook the hands of the condemned to ascertain their weight and thus ensure that the long drop would kill them quickly and humanely.

This is almost certainly apocryphal, for such calculations were made professionally, with medically recorded heights and weights. It is, however, the case that executions like this were conducted with merciful speed and a generous measure of liquor, taking no more than two minutes from cell to rope and giving the subject little time to think or struggle.

Cummins was thought likely to have committed two other murders the previous autumn while on leave. On 13 October 1941, the remains of 19-year-old Maple Churchyard were found in a bombed-out house near Charing Cross. She had been strangled with her own underwear and robbed but not sexually assaulted. On 17 October 1941, 48-year-old Edith Humphries was found clinging to life at her home in Regent's Park. She had been beaten and strangled, her throat had been slashed and her skull penetrated, and she died in hospital. She had also been robbed.

Cummins fits the definition of a hedonistic serial killer. Whether he was conning the world into believing he was an aristocratic heir or an upper-crust fighter pilot, or stalking and murdering women while his loyal wife believed he was enjoying some deserved rest and recuperation, he appears to have been interested solely in his own psychological and physical gratification. The idea that Cummins experienced formative trauma can't be ruled out, and it may be that being sent away to boarding school at a young age left its mark. Perhaps he took one lesson too much to heart: to best look after one's self in the closed, potentially hostile society of a boarding school, a child should learn to charm, manipulate and exploit those around them.

Until his antisocial behaviour became murderous and chaotic in 1941 and 1942, Cummins was highly organized and sustained both a superficially happy marriage and a worthwhile military career alongside his fantasy life. Delusion or ideology may have informed his violence, which did betray a savage degree of misogyny, but he took the truth of his state of mind to the grave.

JEFFREY DAHMER: THE MILWAUKEE MONSTER

Between 1978 and 1991, Jeffrey Dahmer murdered 17 men and children in the states of Ohio and Wisconsin in the US Midwest. He was a hedonistic serial killer distinguished by the extremity of his paraphilia. Once he'd hit his stride as a murderer, he practised both necrophilia and cannibalism, and dismembered and retained parts of his victims for the purposes of sexual and psychological gratification.

Jeffrey Dahmer was born in Milwaukee, Wisconsin, in 1960 to Lionel Dahmer and Joyce Dahmer. His parents are not believed to have been physically abusive towards their son, and, while their various preoccupations and neuroses may have deprived him of attention, other sources suggest he was well cared for. It has also been suggested that abdominal surgery at the age of four turned Jeffrey from happy and outgoing to timid and self-absorbed. If that medical procedure did indeed cause permanent neurological or physiological change, there has never been an explanation of how it did so.

Lionel Dahmer was often away building a career as a research chemist, while Joyce tried and sometimes failed to balance motherhood and work with mental illness. Joyce suffered from hypochondria, anxiety and depression, was sometimes bedridden or otherwise disengaged from her family and the wider world, and attempted suicide at least once. Jeffrey is not thought to have repeatedly tortured living animals – one possible precursor to serial violence – but he did become fascinated with dead animals, specifically with the inner workings of mortal bodies. His father unwittingly laid the ground for later horror by inspiring and later supporting his son's interest.

At the age of four, Jeffrey saw Lionel removing animal bones from beneath their home and became fascinated by their appearance and texture, and by the noise they made when rubbed together. By the age of eight, he'd become a novice anatomist, seeking out animal skeletons and examining living ones in forensic detail. Later, he preserved small mammals in formaldehyde and, with the help of his father, bleached carcasses to remove soft tissue and preserve bones. He routinely dissected roadkill and memorialized their buried remains with crosses and skulls, and on at least one occasion decapitated a dead dog and displayed its remains in order to enjoy a friend's reaction.

Dahmer had high-functioning alcoholism from early adolescence and became accustomed to spending his waking hours in a haze of indifference. While he was superficially polite and highly intelligent, he underachieved at school and was perhaps typically remembered by his classmates for drinking beer and liquor throughout the school day. Dahmer's parents may not have known the extent of their son's drink problem and were also ignorant of something he had realized in his early teens: he was gay. While he was reticent about his sexuality until well into adulthood, his alcohol-fuelled, solitary fantasy life increasingly fixated on scenarios in which he dominated young, submissive males. He later focused his fantasies on the male torso in isolation, a strand of thought that became intertwined with his love of dissection. In an echo of British serial killer Dennis Nilsen (see Chapter Four), there was an aspect of aesthetic gratification in Dahmer's pathology.

Dahmer completed high school in 1978, the year in which his parents divorced, leaving him alone in the family home. This unhappy, heavy-drinking and disaffected 18-year-old celebrated his independence and found his grim vocation within weeks of graduation. On 18 June, Dahmer saw Steven Hicks, 18, hitchhiking bare-chested in Bath, Ohio. The sight piqued Dahmer's sexual interest and he offered to take Steven home for a few drinks. It soon became clear, however, that Steven was heterosexual and unlikely to accept Dahmer's advances. How much premeditation preceded what followed is debatable. Dahmer would claim, in this and other cases, that he simply didn't want his guest to leave. It is likely that, on this and other occasions, Dahmer knew that a dead and thereby utterly passive and easily posed young man was in fact the perfect date, and one that could be enjoyed in many ways. Steven was beaten unconscious with a dumbbell, choked to death with the dumbbell handle and stripped. Dahmer then luxuriated in the freedom to explore the dead youth's chest without objection or interruption, then became sexually aroused and abused the body.

Six weeks later, Lionel Dahmer and his new fiancée moved into the family home in Bath. He was surprised to find his son there, having believed he'd gone to Wisconsin with his mother. By this time, Jeffrey had thoroughly enjoyed and disposed of Steven Hicks's body. He had dissected and examined the cadaver in the basement, buried it for a while, then disinterred it and carved the flesh from the bones. Next, he had dissolved the flesh in acid and disposed of the viscous solution via the lavatory. He had dried the bones, pulverized them with a sledgehammer and discarded them in woodland. A few personal effects and the dissection tools went into the Cuyahoga River.

Dahmer was soon after prevailed upon to leave the family home. He drank away his university career and dropped out after one unproductive semester. In January 1979, he enlisted in the US Army, where some rough justice temporarily moderated his alcoholism. Under training in Texas, Dahmer responded to an order with drunken insolence and the training officer's response was to punish his entire platoon. In line with military tradition, Dahmer's unhappy comrades passed the punishment to its rightful owner and beat him severely enough to curb his drinking for a time. Dahmer did become a somewhat effective combat medic, serving in both the USA and Germany in a role that may have dovetailed well with his anatomical insights. By early 1981, however, his drinking was out of control again and he was discharged back into civilian life. By the autumn of that year, he had returned to the Midwest to live initially with his father and later with his grandmother. His alcohol consumption at that time was so extreme that everything he earned was spent on it, obliging relatives to support him.

While there appears to have been a lengthy hiatus between Dahmer's first murder in 1978 and his next in 1987, there were still worrying signs that his demons hadn't gone away. He was arrested for indecently exposing himself at the Wisconsin State Fair Park in August 1982. In 1985, he refused an offer of fellatio from a stranger in a library but his sexual self was reawakened and he sought to express it. Unfortunately, Dahmer's sexuality was still fixed on his formative fantasies of dominating passive subjects. He explored the gay scene of Milwaukee and stole a male mannequin, whose torso served as a sex object for Dahmer until his grandmother forced him to dispose of it. He also sought out sexual encounters at bathhouses but deplored the fact that his partners moved of their own volition. They were, after all, sex objects and objects should be inanimate.

In September 1986, Dahmer was arrested for masturbating close to children on a riverbank. He received probation and mandatory counselling for an offence that was as nothing compared to his other activities. Not only had he dishonestly obtained sedatives and routinely slipped them into the drinks of his sexual partners to render them unconscious, but also he had tried and failed to disinter a recently dead 18-year-old male for sexual purposes. Dahmer would later claim that his first murder of the 1980s happened in a fit of drunken absent-mindedness. On 20 November 1987, he met Steven Tuomi, 25, in a bar and invited him back to his hotel room. His non-lethal modus operandi of sedating the subject and using his passive body at his leisure had gone awry, for Dahmer woke next to a dead man with a crushed chest. He covertly transported the body to his grandmother's house and treated it much as he had treated Steven Hicks's remains save for a few variations. Most of Steven Tuomi's remains went to the city dump with the rest of the household waste, save for the head, which was boiled in detergent so that Dahmer could keep the skull as a masturbatory aid.

From this point on, Dahmer ceased trying to control or redirect his demons. He would go on to inflict his vision of lethal sexual fulfilment on a total of 17 men and boys. Oblivious to the fact that Dahmer had already killed four times, on 23 April 1988 Ronald Flowers Jr was persuaded to accompany Dahmer to his grandmother's house and was given a sedative-laced drink. As Dahmer prepared to use and dispose of Ronald, his grandmother called out, asking if somebody was in the house and receiving a reply that convinced her that her grandson was home and had brought company. This obliged Dahmer to drive an unconscious but alive Ronald to hospital and abandon him there.

Dahmer's grandmother evicted him in September 1988. The stench of decay from the basement was insufferable and the drunken parade of late-night sexual partners was disturbing. Within days of moving into a one-bedroom apartment, Dahmer was arrested for drugging and sexually abusing a 13-year-old lured there ostensibly for a photo session. Lionel Dahmer sprang to his son's defence and paid for a defence attorney, who requested court-sanctioned psychological assessments. The court heard that, inter alia, Jeffrey suffered from schizoid personality disorder, manifesting in a rich internal fantasy life contrasting with a stunted external life that was solitary, detached and apathetic. Between pleading guilty to sexual assault in January 1989 and being sentenced to probation in May 1989, Dahmer murdered Anthony Sears, 24, at his grandmother's house, using her bath to flay the flesh from the bones and preserving the head and genitals in acetone for later abuse.

Dahmer had killed five times by May 1989 and was known to the police, the probation service and the sex offenders register. Remarkably, however, the worst was yet to come. In May 1990, he left his grandmother's house again and moved to an address he would make infamous, Apartment 213 at 924 North 25th Street, Milwaukee. Within a week, Dahmer had killed his sixth victim, 32-year-old sex worker Raymond Smith. Having full control of his own private residence led Dahmer to take even more time with his abuse and dissections. He acquired a Polaroid camera so that he could photograph his dismemberments step by step, together with a large container in which flesh was dissolved in acid. Raymond Smith's skull joined Anthony Sears's in Dahmer's home-made ossuary.

Around 27 May 1990, Dahmer was robbed by an unknown man who luckily escaped becoming his seventh victim. Dahmer accidentally drugged himself and woke up alone and without his watch and cash. It is a measure of his detachment from reality that Dahmer complained about the theft to his probation officer. Dahmer murdered 27-year-old Edward Smith in June but botched the preservation process for his skull, leading him to regard the killing as wasteful. In September, 22-year-old Ernest Miller became the eighth victim and had his throat slashed because Dahmer was running low on sedatives. Dahmer was adapting and refining his modus operandi with every kill. He severed Ernest Miller's head so that he could kiss it and make consoling small talk while he worked on the body. The head would later be enamelled, while organs and muscles were frozen to be eaten later. Dahmer dispatched his ninth victim, David Thomas, 22, a few weeks later, then didn't kill again for nearly five months.

Dahmer murdered his final eight victims in a six-month spree between February and July 1991. Seven of them were young, adult males, but one was only 14 years old. On 27 May, teenager Konerak Sinthasomphone was lured into Apartment 213 by Dahmer having been promised cash to pose for pictures. While drugged but still conscious, Konerak was shown the body of Tony Hughes, killed three days before. Dahmer, in an experimental mood, then drilled a hole through Konerak's skull and injected hydrochloric acid into his brain. Remarkably, the boy survived and one of the most disturbing chapters in Dahmer's story unfolded.

Dahmer had gone out drinking and left Konerak alone. When he returned, he found Konerak on the street near his apartment block, naked and talking in Lao to three bystanders who had called the police. When the officers appeared, Dahmer told them that Konerak was his boyfriend, with whom he'd had a drunken argument. To the disgust of the bystanders, the officers seemed to believe him. Paramedics then arrived, gave the Lao youth a perfunctory check and a blanket and left. The officers then escorted Dahmer and Konerak to Apartment 213, where they were shown Polaroids of the youth in supposedly erotic poses. Despite the unholy stench of faeces, blood and decomposition that permeated the dwelling, the officers then left, urging Dahmer to take good care of Konerak. Dahmer did just that, by his own standards at least: having miraculously escaped his murderer's abattoir, the boy was returned there by law enforcement and promptly dispatched by Dahmer with a second acid injection to the brain.

The viscerally repugnant state of Apartment 213 during the summer of 1991 cannot be exaggerated. Mortuary technicians perform post-mortem examinations in clinical settings built with hygiene, drainage and ventilation in mind; even there, a bystander wearing a mask and goggles will still smell blood, fat and excrement. The use of electric cutting tools adds a fine, pungent mist of heated and atomized blood, bone and sinew. Throughout 1991, Dahmer performed numerous amateur dissections of humans in a one-bedroom apartment. Not only was every surface in that space saturated with human fluids and organic decay, but so were the communal ventilation system and drains. The fridge, freezer and a 216-litre (57-gallon) vat of acid were also stuffed with body parts.

This miasma of dread greeted the police officers who returned Konerak Sinthasomphone to Hell in May 1991. It also greeted Tracy Edwards, 32, on 22 July 1991 when he narrowly escaped becoming Dahmer's eighteenth victim. Tracy had accepted an offer of US$100 to pose for nude photographs but immediately noticed the stench and several containers of acid when he entered Apartment 213. As the two men made nervous small talk, Dahmer tried and failed to handcuff Tracy, applying a bracelet to just one wrist. In the bedroom, Tracy went into survival mode: when Dahmer produced a knife and stated his intention to take pictures, Tracy agreed provided that Dahmer put the knife down and uncuffed him. Dahmer briefly resumed watching a favourite movie on his TV, *The Exorcist III*, while rocking and mumbling to himself. He then produced the knife again, rested his ear on Tracy's chest and stated that he was going to eat the heart to which he was listening.

Tracy repeatedly told Dahmer that he was his friend and wasn't about to run out on him. Eventually, Dahmer became distracted and Tracy took his chance, punching his would-be murderer to the floor and running from Apartment 213. His ordeal had lasted an estimated five hours. On the street, Tracy flagged down two police officers and explained what had happened. Their police-issue handcuff keys didn't fit the single cuff attached to Tracy's wrist. They took Tracy back to Dahmer's dwelling, ostensibly to ask for the right key. Dahmer allowed the officers entry and told them the handcuff key was in a bedroom drawer. An officer insisted on retrieving it himself and noticed, in addition to the unavoidable stench, a large knife and Polaroid pictures of a victim in multiple stages of dismemberment. Dahmer realized the game was up and tried and failed to overpower the officers. As he lay face down on the floor, handcuffed behind his back, he is alleged to have said "for what I did, I should be dead."

Over 60 hours of police interviews, Dahmer willingly and vividly admitted each and every one of his murders. He told detectives that he had been responsible for horror and believed that confessing all was the right thing to do. There was such an abundance of physical evidence at his home that one investigator likened it to a murder museum. For legal purposes, Dahmer was held to be sane, albeit affected by MPDs. He pleaded guilty and directly addressed the court, stating that he deserved the maximum sanction and expected no consideration. He was sentenced to 16 consecutive terms of life imprisonment. On 28 November 1994, Dahmer was beaten to death by fellow inmate Christopher Scarver, a schizophrenic killer who told guards that he'd carried out God's instructions.

Jeffrey Dahmer is generally regarded as a hedonistic serial killer. He appears to have lived in a self-absorbed, semi-inebriated haze, dissociated from any sense of moral inhibition or empathy and devoted to fulfilling his dominant fantasy, one in which young men were just sets of body parts to be collected, dominated, posed, appreciated, abused and dissected. One court-appointed psychiatrist stated that Dahmer had killed because his victims symbolized an aspect of his own personality that he hated.

JOHN WAYNE GACY: THE KILLER CLOWN

Coulrophobia is loosely defined as the irrational fear of clowns. The word is a neologism and describes a cultural phenomenon rather than a recognized psychiatric disorder. While many in the Western world find the appearance of clowns unsettling, this arguably owes more to fiction and folklore than it does to clinical reality. Some commentators observe similarities between clown costumes and stereotypical images of demons, while others point to the "uncanny valley" effect, whereby objects or costumes create fearful uncertainty by almost but not quite resembling humans.

Clowns have a rich heritage. There was, for example, the medieval tradition of the motley fool – also but inaccurately known as the court jester – whose prerogative was to deliver uncomfortable truths without fear of retribution. In contemporary Western culture, however, the clown has become a sinister staple of ghost trains, superhero comics and horror fiction, most distinctly in Stephen King's *It*. Fiction aside, the latter-day killer-clown stereotype may owe much of its power and resonance to one of history's cruellest serial killers: John Wayne Gacy.

During the 1970s, John Wayne Gacy was devoted to his alter ego, Pogo the Clown, a jovial, wise-cracking, costumed magician who hosted neighbourhood street parties and cheered up poorly children in hospitals. Between 1972 and 1978, Gacy also raped, tortured and murdered 33 men and children in Iowa and Illinois in the US Midwest. Many were persuaded to join him at his home in Norwood Park Township near Chicago and put on handcuffs so that he could demonstrate his close-up magic.

Gacy was born in Chicago in March 1942 to John Stanley Gacy, a mechanic and veteran of the First World War, and Marion Elaine Robison, a homemaker. John Stanley was a hard-drinking bully who physically abused John Wayne, then verbally abused him as an effeminate mother's boy when his mother stepped in to protect him. At the age of seven, John Wayne was whipped by his father when he was caught sexually assaulting a young girl. From around the same time, he was himself sexually abused by a family friend, but never dared to tell his parents. John Wayne grew up overweight and unathletic and was periodically hospitalized in his teens for various health problems. While he had every reason to resent his father, his response was less straightforward. John Wayne appears to have revered John Stanley and internalized his father's opinions of him. This would have dire consequences.

Gacy's dysfunctional relationship with his father persisted into adulthood. At the age of 18 in 1960, he began working as an assistant precinct captain for his local Democratic Party. Given his unhappy, disrupted childhood, this was something of an achievement, but earned him only politically partisan derision from his father. The old man also bought Gacy a car but wouldn't let him use it without permission until he'd paid for it and clipped his son's wings by keeping the keys or removing a vital component.

In 1962, Gacy finally fled the family home and moved to Las Vegas. There he made his first acquaintance with the dead and was frightened by his own response. While working as a mortuary assistant, he became accustomed to handling the dead and seeing how morticians worked. One evening while sleeping alone at the mortuary, he followed a whim by joining a young male cadaver in its coffin and caressing it lovingly.

Gacy returned to Chicago shortly thereafter and became career-minded. After studying at business college, he worked in retail management and discovered a talent for selling. He relished his power to talk anyone into doing anything and initially used it for nothing more sinister than selling clothing or chicken dinners. In 1966, he married Marlynn Myers, with whom he had two children, and secured a highly paid role running his father-in-law's fast-food franchises. This inspired John Stanley to apologize to John Wayne for getting his son so wrong.

John Wayne Gacy was not set to embrace his bullying father's vision for a worthwhile life, however, and set out to lead a double life. The wholesome family man was well regarded for his charity work for the local chapter of the Jaycees, a civic organization. Yet Gacy and fellow members misused the Jaycees to coordinate drug abuse, swinging and the use of sex workers. Gacy was grappling with his sexual identity while embracing a coercive approach to sex. He persuaded, bribed and blackmailed several teenage boys into submitting to sexual abuse and ultimately word got out. He was arrested and charged with both sexually assaulting a 15-year-old boy and hiring another youth to violently intimidate that boy into withholding evidence.

In 1968, Gacy was jailed for sexual assault, having been diagnosed with antisocial personality disorder by court-appointed psychiatrists. He was sentenced to ten years' incarceration and his cookie-cutter vision of the perfect life was in ruins. Marlynn Myers divorced him and Gacy never saw her or his children again. Unfortunately for 33 men and boys, Gacy had developed strong powers of optimism and manipulation during his brief sales career. He became a model prisoner, working hard to improve his own lot and that of his fellow inmates. When he faced his second parole hearing in June 1970, he was head cook, had improved motivation and conditions for working prisoners and had earned his high-school diploma. Remarkably, Gacy was released on probation only 18 months into a ten-year sentence. He returned to Chicago and lived with his now widowed mother, John Stanley having died of liver cirrhosis, a loss mourned by Gacy loudly and publicly.

Gacy bounced back remarkably well, marrying again, setting up a thriving construction business and, with financial help from his mother, buying the ranch-style house that would become notorious: 8213 West Summerdale Avenue, Norwood Park Township, Chicago. He also succumbed to cruel sexual compulsions that steadily escalated towards multiple murders, all of which might have been prevented but for bureaucratic failures. Twice in 1971, Gacy was charged with sexual assault on minors involving force or coercion. Both charges foundered due to uncooperative witnesses, but it is significant that the parole board responsible for Gacy did not learn of them before they sealed his 1968 convictions.

By luck and selling ability, Gacy had freed himself from the consequences of his crimes and begun to turn himself into a respected pillar of the community again. During the 1970s, he remained involved with the Jaycees, became a precinct captain for the local Democratic Party – he was photographed in 1978 with US First Lady Rosalynn Carter – and created two alter egos, Pogo the Clown and Patches the Clown. Pogo was happy and Patches was sombre, and both performed at street parties, political junkets and children's hospitals. Behind the make-up and the party badge, however, Gacy was indulging his cruellest appetites.

There was an early indication that something was awry in 1973. An employee of Gacy's business appeared at his home address and beat him up in the front garden. Gacy told his then wife that it was nothing more than a dispute over payment for a poor job of work. It later emerged that the man had been taken to Florida by Gacy to assess a construction project; while staying in a hotel, he had been raped by Gacy. Similar accounts would be heard in the reckoning that followed Gacy's arrest and conviction, all from young male employees of Gacy who had either been raped by him or successfully fought back against rape attempts.

Tragically, 33 men and boys didn't live to share their testimonies, and many of their remains would be found in the crawl space beneath 8213 West Summerdale Avenue. Gacy used his company – PDM – as both bait and a source of victims: he offered jobs to lure victims or targeted young men who already worked for him. Sometimes he was acquainted with his victims and sometimes he found them on the streets of Chicago. He is known to have carried a bogus sheriff's badge and installed spotlights on his car so that he could pretend to work in law enforcement. Intended murder victims were generally taken to Gacy's home, where he would use professional bonhomie as well as drink and drugs to soften their defences.

A signature part of Gacy's modus operandi was a grisly echo of the comic timing and sleight of hand he used in his clowning. He would offer to demonstrate a magic trick, first handcuffing himself behind his back and then magically releasing himself to show how harmless and easy it was. His victims didn't know when they agreed to be similarly cuffed that Gacy had released himself with a palmed key. They would then be subjected to a battery of abuse, rape and torture, including forced fellatio, various forms of penetration, endless mockery, choking and harsh restraint. Even the coup de grâce was slow and maximally sadistic: a rope tourniquet around the neck would be tightened incrementally so that death could take hours. Most were buried beneath Gacy's house with quicklime to speed up decomposition.

Accounts of how Gacy's victims died came from him and, as he was a habitual liar and manipulator, should be treated with caution. It is sufficient to say that they all suffered appallingly and their lives were snuffed out with diabolically intense malice. The first confirmed victim was 16-year-old Timothy McCoy, taken from Chicago's main bus terminal on 3 January 1972. After killing this boy at 8213 West Summerdale Avenue and burying him in the crawl space, Gacy allegedly decided that killing delivered an incomparable thrill. The second confirmed victim was dispatched in January 1974 and remains unidentified at the time of writing. The third confirmed victim was 18-year-old John Butkovich, an employee of Gacy's killed on 31 July 1975 after demanding an overdue payment.

It was reported that John's parents called law enforcement more than 100 times urging them to look into Gacy.

Gacy's second divorce was concluded in March 1976, after which the pace of his killing increased markedly. Between 6 April 1976 and 11 December 1978, he murdered 26 identified men and children. The first victim in what became known as Gacy's cruising period – so named for his habit of openly cruising the streets in his car in search of sex – was 18-year-old Darrell Samson, and the last was 15-year-old Robert Piest. In the same period, he murdered five young males, who, to date, remain unidentified despite the fact that facial reconstructions were issued to the media. Between these stark facts lies an ocean of pain and heartbreak, punctuated by institutional failures. Yet Gacy was pushing his luck and his run of killings was nearing its end.

Gacy murdered Gregory Godzik, 17, on 12 December 1976. Gregory worked for Gacy and had told his family that he'd been asked to do some building work under his boss's home. When Gregory's family made frantic enquiries about their missing son, Gacy extemporized feebly, claiming that the boy had expressed a sudden desire to run away from home and had left an answerphone message to this effect, although this had sadly been erased. On 20 January 1977, Gacy invited John Szyc, 19, to his home on the basis that he wanted to buy the youth's car, a Plymouth Satellite. Gacy killed the youth, appropriated the car, registered it to himself and later disposed of it. In April 1977, Szyc's car was used in petty crime and traced back to Gacy, who explained that the young man had sold the car to him for cash as he needed to leave town urgently. The police appeared oblivious to the emerging pattern and no further action was taken. It should be noted that, between each one of these incidents, other murders were taking place.

Gacy's murders during 1977 included Robert Gilroy, 18, the son of a Chicago police officer. On 30 December 1977, yet another missed opportunity followed a lucky escape. Robert Donnelly, 19, was abducted by Gacy at gunpoint, then raped, tortured and repeatedly drowned to unconsciousness while begging for death. Gacy refused to kill him until it suited him, but then abruptly decided to spare the youth, releasing him with a warning that he would not be believed if he reported his ordeal. While this appears at first glance to be complacency or hubris on Gacy's part, he was correct in his low opinion of local law enforcement. Robert Donnelly did approach the police, who questioned Gacy and believed him when he said the sex was consensual and the youth was bitter because he hadn't been paid. No charges were proffered and it appears that Gacy spared Robert not out of mercy but for the thrill of manipulating both the youth and law enforcement.

This new aspect of Gacy's offending was repeated on 21 March 1978. Jeffrey Rignall, 26, was abducted, raped and tortured using a home-made pillory, then chloroformed and dumped unconscious but alive in a public park. The incident was reported to the local police, who declined to investigate. Jeffrey and his friends took matters into their own hands and staked out local roads, looking for Gacy's car. In April, they finally saw it and followed it back to 8213 West Summerdale. The police were finally pressured into acting and in July 1978 Gacy was charged with assaulting Jeffrey Rignall.

By this point, Gacy's crawl space could accommodate no more cadavers and he had begun dumping remains into the

Des Plaines River. On 11 December 1978, the mother of 15-year-old Robert Piest drove to collect her son from the Des Plaines pharmacy where he worked part-time. Robert told her he had to briefly leave the store, as a contractor wanted to talk to him about a job offer, adding that he wouldn't be long and asking her to wait. She never saw her son again. Gacy was known to have visited that pharmacy to discuss building work and to have mentioned that he employed teenage boys and paid well. Robert Piest would die a lonely, anguished death, but there would finally be consequences for Gacy.

The Piest family reported their son missing and the Des Plaines Police Department began putting the pieces together. Not only was Gacy a plausible last contact for Robert Piest, but a background check showed a previous conviction for sexual assault and a charge for assault, both against young males. Gacy was visited at his home, insisted he hadn't offered Robert a job and undertook to come to the station voluntarily to make a statement. When asked to attend sooner rather than later, he accused the officers of lacking respect for the dead, a non sequitur that must have set alarm bells ringing. Gacy attended the police station several times, the first time in the early hours while manic and covered in mud. He was prevailed upon to prepare a thorough statement of his movements on 11 December. Inviting a suspect to give a detailed account is a sound investigative tactic. It is informally likened to giving a suspect enough rope with which to hang themselves, for only a truly gifted liar can give a detailed but dishonest account while excluding contradictions and inconsistencies.

Over the next few weeks, police searched the interior of Gacy's home, began piecing together the connections between him and missing youths and surveilled him around the clock. While he still fancied himself the master manipulator, desperation began to dog his heels. On 18 December 1978, he invited two detectives to breakfast and tried to charm them but couldn't resist bragging that clowns can get away with murder. Later that day, he instructed his lawyers to sue the police for harassment. In the meantime, officers were preparing a search warrant, having learned that trenches had been dug and quicklime spread beneath Gacy's home. Despite Gacy's attempts to delay the inevitable by unplugging a pump and partially flooding the crawl space, crime-scene investigators found human remains within minutes of beginning their excavations below the monster's home.

In the bleak Illinois midwinter of 1979 into 1980, 29 bodies were recovered from 8213 West Summerdale along with an array of evidence of predation and torture. Gacy confessed to all the murders he could remember, with the craven caveat that all had entered his home willingly. On 6 February 1980, Gacy was charged with 33 murders and sent for trial. His defence team made an unsuccessful insanity plea. In his opening address to the jury, attorney Robert Motta said, inter alia, that the defence of insanity had to be valid because "if Gacy is normal, then our concept of normality is totally distorted." This is powerful and intuitive and could play well with a jury but it is legally disingenuous; as Gacy was aware of and in control of his actions, and knew the difference between right and wrong, he was capable of forming the requisite intent for murder. Gacy was found guilty on all charges and sentenced to death.

Gacy was a demonically hedonistic serial killer. He is believed to have suffered from antisocial personality disorder caused by trauma in his youth. He killed because his sexuality was warped by aggression and repression, because he had detached himself from social norms, because he was barely capable of remorse or empathy and, most of all, because he enjoyed it. When the serial killer known to friends and neighbours as Pogo the Clown was executed by lethal injection in May 1994, he offered a final punchline characteristically lacking in wit, grace and remorse: "Kiss my ass!"

ZODIAC: THE CIPHER KILLER

Hedonistic serial killers are generally defined by the pleasure they derive from the physical act of killing. They horrify because of their predilection for torture as a means of extracting the maximum pain and fear from their victims. One hedonistic killer added a distinct variation to this pattern. He is unidentified and may well remain so in perpetuity, but his nom de guerre is infamous: Zodiac.

Fictional serial-killer thrillers often feature impossibly elaborate puzzles set by the murderer for maverick, genius detectives to solve. While some categories of serial killer may be organized, cunning and forensically aware, the trope of the mastermind murderer is a fantasy. Zodiac was, however, the closest reality ever got to this idea. This very particular hedonist drew his greatest pleasure not from his murders but from his systematic and sustained battle of wits with law enforcement and the media.

Between December 1968 and October 1969, Zodiac killed five people in San Francisco and the Napa Valley in California, USA, and gravely injured two more. Between July 1969 and January 1974, he sent numerous letters and ciphers to both law enforcement and newspapers, calling himself Zodiac. He also sent four cryptograms, of which two have been solved to date. Zodiac's missives were generally badly spelled and unilluminating and amounted to self-satisfied gloating. Many were signed with a symbol resembling the cross hairs of a gunsight.

The first murders positively attributed to Zodiac took place in Bernicia in the Bay Area of San Francisco on the evening of 20 December 1968. High-school sweethearts Betty Jensen, 16, and David Faraday, 17, were sitting together in David's car on a secluded track known locally as a lovers' lane. Their killer fired numerous shots into the car, not hitting either Betty or David. Their luck was short-lived, however. David was shot in the head as he exited his car, while Betty was shot five times in the back as she tried to flee. The motiveless malevolence of the crime shocked the Bay Area community and baffled the police. Not only did the killer lack an obvious motive, but he had left no evidence behind. There was also nothing to indicate that these were serial killings.

Zodiac bided his time and struck again in the early hours of 4 July 1969 in Vallejo in the Bay Area. Late on the evening of 3 July, Darlene Ferrin, 22, picked up Michael Mageau, 19, and drove him to a lovers' lane location only a few miles from the scene of the December killings. They were followed by a man in a car who stopped near them. He later approached Darlene's car, shining a torch into their eyes and leading the couple to believe he was a police officer. Both Darlene and Michael were then shot multiple times with a handgun.

Darlene died in hospital and Michael survived and provided a description; neither that description nor any crime-scene evidence helped to provide a motive or a suspect. Shortly after the attack, however, Zodiac made a brief call to the police from a payphone; he claimed responsibility for that night's and December's shootings, although he offered no other useful information. Zodiac would develop and greatly elaborate both of these characteristics: the urgent need to take credit and the careful withholding of anything that might assist law enforcement.

Soon after the murder of Darlene Ferrin, Zodiac began his lengthy, anonymous letter campaign. Three San Francisco newspapers received similar letters on 1 August 1969. Each one claimed responsibility for the December and July killings and enclosed a cipher made up of 408 symbols. The writer threatened to spend the next weekend killing people unless the ciphers were published on the front pages. When the *San Francisco Chronicle* published its share of the cryptic symbols, an accompanying article penned by Vallejo's police chief expressed scepticism and urged the mysterious correspondent to share more details to confirm his bona fides.

In early August, the killer began introducing himself as "Zodiac" in his letters. He also furnished Vallejo's police chief with detail that established his intimate knowledge of the offences while, as usual, withholding anything that might risk his liberty. He also teased that, if the cipher of 1 August were cracked, he would be identified; this turned out to be nonsense. In all probability, few expected that cipher to be cracked any time soon, Zodiac included. The FBI and the CIA allegedly tried and failed but were upstaged by amateur puzzlers Bettye and Donald Harden of Salinas, California, who cracked it on 5 August. They devised a crib – a code-breaking device based on characteristic patterns formed by language – on the assumption that the word "kill" would feature heavily. They also assumed that the killer was egocentric and that the first letter would be "I".

The first cracked Zodiac cipher contained nothing that would definitively identify him and few psychological insights beyond what had been gleaned from his modus operandi, uncoded correspondence included. Zodiac rejoiced in the fun of killing, likening it to hunting dangerous game and finding it better than sex. His killings, he believed, would ensure that he was reborn in paradise with his victims as his enslaved people. He clearly stated that he would not be disclosing his real name.

Zodiac appeared to be revelling in his assumed identity and devised a costume to go with it. On the afternoon of 27 September 1969, Bryan Hartnell, 20, and Cecelia Shepard, 22, were picnicking at Lake Berryessa in Napa Valley when they were approached from the treeline by an oddly dressed man. The figure sported a black hood, clip-on sunglasses and a bib bearing Zodiac's signature symbol, the cross hairs from a gunsight. Bryan and Cecelia were threatened with a handgun and told that their car and their money would be taken, as their assailant had absconded from jail and was fleeing to Mexico. Zodiac then made the couple tie each other up and then stabbed them both multiple times.

Rather than taking Bryan Hartnell's car, Zodiac used a felt-tip pen to record his symbol and the dates of his murders up to that point on one of its doors. He also left footprints and eyewitnesses. Both Bryan Hartnell and Cecelia Shepard gave initial descriptions of their attacker; Cecelia died in hospital but Bryan lived to give a detailed account. A consistent if frustratingly commonplace physical picture of Zodiac was emerging: a stocky white man, around 1.8 m (6 ft) in height, with light-brown hair. The Lake Berryessa attack also elicited a composite sketch of the killer's face. Zodiac drove from the lake to a payphone in Napa and phoned in another anonymous confession, in the process leaving a good palm print that has, to date, not been matched to anyone.

Zodiac's last confirmed murder was staged on the evening of 11 October 1969 in San Francisco. He hailed a taxi that was being driven by Paul Stine, 29 – a student working to support his studies – and asked to be driven to Presidio Heights. Near the junction of Washington and Cherry, Zodiac produced a handgun and shot Paul fatally in the head. Several teenage witnesses in a nearby house heard the gunshot, called the police and watched as the killer searched his victim, stole his valuables, tried to wipe away forensic evidence and left the scene.

The few minutes after a teenage witness in Presidio Heights dialled 911 were the closest Zodiac ever came to justice. Had the police dispatcher not botched their radio message, then the Zodiac legend might just be a forgotten eccentricity of a convicted murderer. A patrol car responded within two minutes of the 911 call but the officers had been told that the suspect was Black. In fact, the caller had described a white man in a dark or black top, and the officers did in fact stop and speak to such a man, who took the time to misdirect the officers, claiming to have seen someone waving a gun and heading in the opposite direction. Zodiac later called to confirm his latest killing, adding that he had spoken to San Francisco Police Department (SFPD) officers immediately after murdering Paul Stine.

Both the teenage witnesses and the two SFPD patrol officers helped to generate two near-identical and definitive sketches of Zodiac. They described a white man with short, neat dark hair, smart spectacles, appraising eyes, a scowl and a thin mouth. To date, there have been no other confirmed sightings. In an interesting sidenote, it seemed that Zodiac's enjoyment of manipulation by letter was contagious. SFPD's Detective Dave Toschi eventually worked the Presidio Heights murder alone and dismissed Zodiac's correspondence as an act of egotism. In 1978, however, Toschi was demoted after sending anonymous letters to the *San Francisco Chronicle* praising his own work. When the same publication received another possible letter from Zodiac later that year, the SFPD had to take steps to confirm that Toschi hadn't written it.

Zodiac has not been definitively linked to any murders after 11 October 1969 but did persist with his vainglorious correspondence for several years. This vanity campaign inspired many fictional serial killers and at least one imitator. On 22 October 1969, a psychiatric patient named Eric Weill called a TV show pretending to be Zodiac and claiming that he was too afraid of execution to reveal his identity. On 8 November 1969, a 340-character Zodiac cryptogram was published by the *San Francisco Chronicle* and remained opaque until December 2020, when an international group of hobbyists with mathematical and computing acumen cracked it. Remarkable as this achievement was, any hope that Zodiac would share anything meaningful was predictably thwarted. He insisted he hadn't called in to any TV show and in any case didn't fear the death penalty, as he now had enough dead enslaved people to tend to him in paradise.

Zodiac's 1970 letter-writing campaign included a 13-character cipher that has never been solved but purports to be his name. He taunted the police and media by denying responsibility for the lethal bombing of a San Francisco police station, then threatening to bomb public transport unless the *San Francisco Chronicle* wrote about his imaginary bombing campaign and unless the general public started wearing Zodiac badges. He may also have set out to win small victories against law enforcement by misdirecting other inquiries and generally wasting their time and resources. Supposedly indignant that the public weren't wearing Zodiac badges, he then claimed to have murdered SFPD's Sergeant Richard Radetich, shot dead during a traffic stop; even though that murder remains unsolved, the SFPD eliminated Zodiac from their enquiries.

Yet another red herring was a map and cipher sent in June 1970 and allegedly showing the location of a buried bomb. The cipher has never been broken and the bomb, if it ever existed at all, was never found. Zodiac completed his 1970 correspondence campaign by sending a threatening Halloween card to *San Francisco Chronicle* journalist Paul Avery. Although Zodiac must have been gratified to see his latest work on the front page, Avery himself declined police protection but did acquire a handgun. In an act of dark humour, Avery's colleagues wore badges proclaiming "I Am Not Avery".

Whatever the underlying pathology, Zodiac didn't communicate at all between March 1971 and his final confirmed letter in January 1974. In that last characteristically obtuse and opaque letter, Zodiac referenced William Friedkin's movie *The Exorcist* and the Gilbert and Sullivan comic opera *The Mikado* and concluded with a scoreline: "Me = 37, SFPD = 0". It was theorized by psychiatrist David Van Nuys that, whomever Zodiac believed himself to be, he may have been afflicted by MPD. MPD is characterized by two distinct, enduring and fully formed personalities cohabiting within one individual but dissociated from one another. While there is disagreement in psychiatry about the precise nature and definition of dissociation, for the purposes of Van Nuys's theory it would mean that the Zodiac persona was a walking, talking symptom that could be repressed either temporarily or permanently, thus explaining the episodic nature of both the letters and the murders.

There is a gulf between the tally of five murders officially ascribed to Zodiac and the 37 he claimed. That said, Zodiac appeared more interested in taunting than in killing and wasn't shy about taking credit for his murders. The possibility remains that he killed more than five victims – and a number of unsolved incidents might fit the bill – but the definitive truth is unlikely to emerge. To date, the SFPD has investigated at least 2,500 potential suspects. Of these, no more than a dozen were deemed viable suspects, and the best known was Arthur Leigh Allen.

Allen was born in Hawaii in 1933 but grew up in Vallejo, California. He served in the US Navy in the 1950s and was honourably discharged. In 1960, he graduated from university and went into teaching. He was fired from one school in Fairfield, California, for bringing a firearm to work. In 1968, he was fired from another school in Valley Springs, California, for sexually assaulting children. In 1974, Allen was arrested again for sexually assaulting minors and in 1977 given a suspended sentence and probation.

The case against Allen is tantalizing but ultimately flawed. He became a suspect in 1971 when a friend, Don Cheney, shared his suspicions with law enforcement. Cheney claimed that, in a conversation several years earlier, Allen had indicated a desire to kill couples at lovers' lanes and to emulate Zodiac by attaching a torch to a gun barrel, presumably as a way to dazzle victims, and by writing to the police. The SFPD dismissed Allen as a suspect when neither his fingerprints nor his handwriting matched any material linked to the Zodiac killings. Intriguingly, Michael Mageau picked Allen out of a police line-up in July 1992, but this took place 23 years after he and Darlene Ferrin were shot by Zodiac in Vallejo. One month later, Allen died of heart disease at his Vallejo home at the age of 59.

Whoever Zodiac was, he remains a tantalizing and contradictory puzzle. He claimed to have killed dozens but in all likelihood killed far fewer and patently derived more – and more prolonged – satisfaction from publicly teasing and taunting. His written spelling and grammar were poor but he had enough intellectual wattage to devise fiendish ciphers, one of which took 51 years to break, while others have yet to be broken. Single-use codes are exponentially more difficult to break than they are to set, but even so Zodiac was cryptographically literate.

Zodiac did not gratify his desires with prolonged torture sessions in the manner of the Wests, the Moors Murderers or John Wayne Gacy. Nonetheless, he was a hedonistic serial killer, murdering for pleasure even if much of that pleasure came after the event and was cerebral in nature. What he had in common with more viscerally hedonistic killers was this: he indulged in the egotistical, selfish gratification of personal desires with utter indifference to the suffering of others.

It must be acknowledged that Zodiac's identity, background and motivation remain unknown, although the case remains open. It might be argued that, regardless of Zodiac's mystique and facility with ciphers, he should be considered not a criminal mastermind but a deranged taker of lives with a pathological addiction to taunting. Many have heard of Zodiac and few could name any of his victims. He wanted lasting fame and has been granted it, and this is the most disturbing aspect of his story.

CHAPTER FOUR:

POWER-ORIENTED SERIAL KILLERS

THE MIND OF A POWER-ORIENTED KILLER

There is a popular notion that wolves lead fiercely hierarchical lives. The fittest dominate and are dubbed "alphas". The weakest are made subservient, lose breeding privileges and are classed as "betas", "deltas" and "gammas". Fur flies and the snow is speckled with blood when these titles are assigned and such is nature's way. This idea has filtered into human identity, encapsulated in the term "alpha male", and crops up often in both corporate and political culture, despite the fact that it grossly oversimplifies both human and wolf societies.

The reality, at least in wolf packs, is more nuanced. Seniority tends to align with age and parenthood as it would in any human family. Cooperation among members of a family group is flexible and geared towards successfully rearing cubs and bringing down prey. Betas, deltas and gammas are free to split off and become alphas in their own family groups. There are, of course, power politics and rivalry within the pack, but hierarchy as a zero-sum game won't help any social animal to survive hard times. If a wolf or human wins such a game, it means that someone else has lost and may well be unhappy about it. Those who are degraded or rendered unhappily subservient won't want to stay that way. And when they seek to put things right, *they might have taken to heart the rules of the zero-sum game and pursue their own form of dominance. Parity will never be enough.*

Power-oriented serial killers are distinguished by the purity of their motivation. Life to them is a zero-sum game: if they are to win then other people will have to lose everything. To secure that victory, they must control and dominate their victims and thereby empower themselves. Some, like Aileen Wuornos and Albert DeSalvo, endured sustained and unimaginable physical or sexual abuse and empowered themselves not by forgiveness or stoicism but by taking ownership of murderous violence and inflicting it on others.

Christopher Wilder delighted not only in raping, killing and torturing young women and children but also in turning some of them into terrified puppets, driving his car while he hunted and abused new victims and, in one case, building up horrifying memories that might one day form a bestselling biography. Israel Keyes's upbringing and training made him a skilled and patient hunter, initially of wild animals and later of people. He was also a stalker, marksman and butcher, all of which, together with his religious indoctrination, may have convinced him that he had a God-given right to exert lethal dominion over lesser mortals. For all that Dr Harold Shipman was a well-regarded family doctor, he is estimated to have killed 218 people over 23 years. Shipman's name doesn't deliver the same visceral tingle of fear or revulsion as names like Dennis Nilsen and Ted Bundy, but he is the most prolific killer within these pages. He derived extraordinary satisfaction from wielding and abusing the power of life and death.

An intriguing feature of power-oriented serial killers is their attitude to police interviews. Harold Shipman did not condescend to share much with law enforcement and took his own life, thus retaining the power of exclusive knowledge. Israel Keyes told investigators only those things he thought they'd be able to work out for themselves, and then in exchange for something he wanted: a fixed execution date.

INSIDE THE MINDS OF SERIAL KILLERS

Ted Bundy was a notoriously chatty and manipulative interview subject, basking in his celebrity and leveraging his killings into a new form of power.

Perhaps there is a gnawing insecurity at the heart of a power-oriented serial killer, a secret fear that, if they aren't winning by the rules they've set for themselves, then they've lost and become nothing more than the sum of their cruelties, perversions and formative traumas. Keep this thought in mind when you delve into the cold, hard minds of these egocentric individuals.

HAROLD SHIPMAN: DEATH-DEALING DOCTOR

At the dawn of the twenty-first century, Harold Shipman, a well-regarded family doctor in Greater Manchester, England, was convicted of the murders of 15 women between 1995 and 1998. In the summer of 2002, a public inquiry concluded that Shipman may well have killed 218 of his patients between 1975 and 1998. It remains the case that there will never be a final, definitive tally of this doctor's serial killing. The uncovering of Shipman's deadly medical practices left a small town traumatized and changed the way British doctors operate, with lasting consequences for those they treat.

If anything about the Shipman case is clear, it is that he had a modus operandi and a victim profile both so distinct and so often repeated that his murders have been seen as re-enactments of a formative experience. The majority of his victims were retired women in good health and were dispatched by injections of strong opiates or the overprescription of other drugs. Whatever else was going on behind the doctor's thick bottle-end glasses and full beard, his offending was neither impulsive nor random.

INSIDE THE MINDS OF SERIAL KILLERS

Consider a teenage boy helplessly watching his mother suffering and dying from lung cancer. Imagine a time when cancer was almost invariably a death sentence, and such a death would take place at home, noisily, angrily, messily and in the heart of family life. Imagine the taboo but nonetheless unavoidable fact of life that unendurable suffering was – and in some places still is – managed and ultimately ended with mercifully generous doses of intravenous morphine from harried family doctors on house calls.

Imagine that teenage boy seeing the doctor slide the needle under the thin, waxen skin of his mother, press the plunger and hold his fingers over her dwindling radial pulse as the pain magically fades from her face and she passes into peaceful oblivion with one long agonal breath of release. Imagine that bright boy rallying, passing all of his exams with impressive grades, heading off to medical school, earning his spurs and becoming a family doctor himself. Imagine the boy inside the man forever reliving those childhood moments of blissful mercy in the family bedroom. Imagine that boy becoming one of history's most prolific serial killers.

Harold Shipman is generally regarded as a power-oriented serial killer. Unlike other killers in this category, he didn't subject his victims to torture and degradation; he may have regarded his hypodermic syringes and high-dose opiates as instruments of pure mercy. He did, however, exert an appalling degree of power over many unfortunate women, making himself the arbiter of life and death. While many of his victims were elderly, most were believed to have been in good health when they lost their lives.

Shipman deviated in another interesting respect from the Hollywood stereotype of power-hungry serial killers. He did not stalk his victims from dense scrubland using camouflaged clothing and night-vision goggles. Instead, he operated brazenly with a bedside manner that made him a popular local figure and a bag of murder implements that happened to be the legitimate tools of his trade. The simple fact that his actions were inconceivable was camouflage enough, up to a point.

Harold Shipman was born in 1946 to working-class, devoutly Methodist parents on a local-authority housing estate in Nottingham in the East Midlands of England. He was 17 years old when he watched his mother succumb to lung cancer, after which he left home to study medicine. In the early 1970s, he moved to West Yorkshire and worked as both a hospital doctor and a general practitioner. Early signs of a problematic relationship with opiates emerged: he developed a drug habit and was caught forging prescriptions for pethidine to feed it. After paying a steep fine and going through rehab, he relocated to Greater Manchester.

From the late 1970s to his arrest and conviction more than 20 years later, Shipman worked mostly in independent practice in the town of Hyde. In March 1998, concerned local doctors reported their suspicions about Shipman to the local coroner. The number of deaths among his patients was out of all proportion to the size of his patient list. Worse, the deceased in question were all fit, retired women and were supposedly discovered by Shipman in their homes, fully dressed and generally alone.

The local police investigated and decided there was insufficient evidence to proceed further. They were later criticized for failing to take seriously what would soon turn out to be one of history's most outrageous sequences of murders. This allowed Shipman to kill three more women before his arrest in September 1998. His final victim was Kathleen Grundy, a former mayor of Hyde and still a vital and well-regarded member of her community. Kathleen's daughter, Angela Woodruff, was a legal professional who was shocked to discover that her mother had supposedly made a will excluding Angela and her children and leaving her estate, valued in excess of £380,000 (more than £700,000 in 2024), to Shipman.

At Woodruff's urging, the police began a more thorough investigation and quickly discovered damning evidence against the dread doctor. Shipman's typewriter was matched to Kathleen Grundy's forged will. Her remains were disinterred and traces found of morphine, for which there had been no verified clinical need. It transpired that Shipman had visited Kathleen Grundy ostensibly to take a blood sample but had instead administered a lethal dose of morphine and endeavoured to steal all her assets.

As was Shipman's wont, he had signed Kathleen Grundy's death certificate and falsified her medical records to create a picture of declining health and morphine addiction. While his modus operandi in Kathleen's murder was typical, his attempt to steal her worldly estate was uncharacteristically reckless. It has been suggested that he was either trying to get caught or contemplating retiring and fleeing the UK.

There are other instances that suggested Shipman's pathological need to kill was spiralling out of control. In December 1997, he murdered Bianka Pomfret, a healthy divorcee only 49 years old, leaving her to be discovered by her son. Shipman created an elaborate and wholly fictitious medical history to justify the levels of morphine found in Bianka's body. Another case involved a moment of grim farce when Shipman turned up at the workplace of one Angela Wagstaff to inform her that her mother, Anne Royal, had died. The dead woman was in fact 81-year-old Kathleen Wagstaff, Angela's mother-in-law, whom Shipman had just murdered.

Hyde endured a grim harvest as human remains were disinterred from various cemeteries under the cover of darkness and forensic tents. While Shipman was charged with and convicted of 15 murders, there is little doubt that the tally was far higher. For the majority of potential victims, however, formal justice would be forever denied. Most British funerals, then as now, were followed immediately by cremation, leaving no physical evidence whatsoever. Even when the deceased are interred, it is vanishingly rare to find useful toxicological evidence after four years or more in the earth; decomposition affects all biological matter over time, and chemical compounds can both degrade and be tainted by other processes of decay. It is worth noting that the cache of evidence seized post-arrest included enough diamorphine to kill 1,500 adults.

What if Shipman's longing to taste the moment of his mother's death overcame cold clinical judgement and professional ethics, time and time again? What if a culture of implicitly trusting a family doctor permitted one of the world's most prolific serial killers to kill a horrifying number of people before their time, all while being welcomed into their homes and praised for his bedside manner?

Dr Harold Shipman deprived dozens of families, criminologists, psychologists and a news-hungry public of the clear answers they all craved. Having been sentenced to life imprisonment by Preston Crown Court in Lancashire in January 2000, Shipman hanged himself in his cell at Wakefield Prison in West Yorkshire in January 2004. His body was cremated out of fear that a marked grave might attract the wrong kind of attention and thereby disturb the peace of yet another cemetery.

Shipman's legacy of anguish endures in Britain. The final report of The Shipman Inquiry in 2005 imposed more stringent controls on how clinicians in the UK use certain drugs. As reported by *The Telegraph* and others, this has allegedly led to doctors under-prescribing pain-relieving drugs to terminally ill patients out of fear of legal consequences, a phenomenon labelled "the Shipman effect".

Gross as his criminal offending was, however, perhaps Shipman's most egregious sin was against the code of ethics to which he as a doctor had pledged himself: to respect human life to the utmost.

AILEEN WUORNOS: ROADSIDE RAGE

On 30 November 1989, while leading a dangerous, degrading life as a sex worker on the highways of Florida, USA, Aileen Wuornos fatally shot 51-year-old Richard Mallory in his car and left his body in scrubland. Up to her arrest in January 1991, Wuornos is believed to have killed a total of seven men presumed to have solicited sex from her, all in similar circumstances. The remains of the seventh victim, Peter Siems, have yet to be found.

During the trial of Aileen Wuornos in 1992, she asserted that she'd killed in self-defence as the dead men had raped her or attempted to. Psychiatrists testified that she had multiple forms of personality disorder, and the defence tried and failed to introduce evidence that Richard Mallory had in the 1950s been charged with assault with intent to rape. Wuornos received six death sentences, spent ten years on death row and was executed by lethal injection in 2002.

Aileen Wuornos lived a thoroughly wretched life. Her parents, Leo Pittman and Diane Wuornos, had married in 1954 in Rochester, Michigan, USA, when he was 18 and she 14. Aileen was born two years later in 1956 but never met her father, as he was convicted of raping a seven-year-old girl and hanged himself in prison. In 1960, Aileen was abandoned by her mother and adopted by her sexually abusive grandfather, who had alcoholism. It is hard to get an accurate sense of how often and from what age Aileen was sexually assaulted, but it is known that at the age of 13 she was raped by a friend of her grandparents and at the age of 14 gave birth to a son who was removed for adoption.

At the age of 15 in 1971, Aileen was evicted by her grandfather and began an itinerant life of sleeping rough, sex work and petty crime. By 1976, Aileen had settled in Florida, where her life took an even more surreal turn: she met and married Lewis Gratz Fell, a well-heeled 69-year-old yacht club president. A few months later, Aileen's rap sheet boasted a few more offences of minor violence and public disorder and her improbable marriage had been annulled. It is telling that, when Aileen's brother died that summer and she received a US$10,000 payment (approximately US$55,000 in 2024) from his insurer, she had no notion of how to buy herself a less chaotic lifestyle. Instead, she burned through the lump sum in months, buying short-lived luxuries including a fancy car that was soon written off.

When she first killed in 1989, Aileen Wuornos had endured 33 years of almost incessant misery and chaos. Since her mid-teens, she had supported herself through sex work and theft, developed alcoholism and attempted suicide multiple times, on one occasion shooting herself in the belly. Aileen was certainly no stranger to firearms: she'd served time in jail for armed robbery in the early 1980s and was later questioned over an allegation that she'd tried to rob a man at gunpoint in his car. In the latter case, the man had almost certainly picked up Aileen for paid sex, raising the possibility that she had robbed other putative clients, who had not felt inclined to report the crime or its circumstances for reputational reasons.

It is therefore hard to be certain what happened on 30 November 1989 when Richard Mallory, a 51-year-old business owner from Clearwater, Florida, picked up Aileen Wuornos on Interstate 75 and drove her to a secluded area. Did he rape her or attempt to do so as alleged by Aileen at trial? He did have a previous conviction for attempted rape. Did she attempt to rob him at gunpoint but met resistance and pulled the trigger? What is known is that Mallory went missing and his body was found several days later and several miles away in woodland, killed by two bullets to the left lung.

While a pattern was to emerge, Aileen was far from a spree killer; Mallory's murder remained an isolated incident for six months. On 19 May 1990, 47-year-old Orange County construction worker David Spears went missing; his stripped body was found on 1 June 1990 on the side of a highway in Citrus County and it was determined that he'd been shot six times with a .22-calibre handgun.

From this point, the pace of Aileen's killing began to pick up and local police piqued the interest of the local, national and global media by declaring that one or possibly two female serial killers were at large. The North Florida city of Ocala found itself hosting reporters from around the world and, in a fascinating twist on the usual serial-killer narrative, it was reported that women were accompanying their male partners on road trips to ensure their safety.

The killings continued. Forty-year-old rodeo worker Charles Carskaddon was shot to death on 31 May 1990 and found a week later. Sixty-five-year-old retired merchant mariner Peter Siems had set out to drive to New Jersey in June 1990 but he never arrived and his body was never found. Fifty-year-old sales executive Troy Burress was reported missing on 31 July 1990 and his body was found in scrubland alongside a highway five days later. Fifty-six-year-old former child-abuse investigator Charles Humphreys was shot in the head on 11 September 1990 and his body found the next day. Finally, the body of 61-year-old security guard and reserve police officer Walter Antonio was found on a logging trail on 19 November 1990.

Wuornos was emphatically not a master criminal. Far from pursuing the perfect murder in the manner of hedonistic killers like Leopold, Loeb, Brady, Hindley and others, Aileen followed up her killings with a degree of reckless abandon that made her arrest inevitable. She was seen driving Charles Carskaddon's car and pawning his gun. She and her romantic partner Tyria Moore were seen abandoning Peter Siems's car; while his body was never found, the fact that his car was recovered with Wuornos's handprint inside it, and that a witness provided a useful description of Wuornos and Moore, would see her tried for his murder.

Eyewitness testimony, a trail of fingerprints left on stolen cars and pawned goods, and a confession elicited from Wuornos by Moore in exchange for immunity led to Wuornos's arrest in January 1991. At her trial, psychiatrists reported that Aileen suffered from both borderline personality disorder and antisocial personality disorder. A typical feature of the former condition is a lifetime of unhealthy and unstable personal relationships, a warped sense of one's identity and intense and unpredictable emotional reactions to both serious and trivial events. The latter is defined by a long-term and active disregard for the feelings and well-being of others and can flow from abusive and alcoholic parenting.

POWER-ORIENTED SERIAL KILLERS

The pathology of Aileen Wuornos as a serial killer has been much debated. Her coarse, defiant, loud-mouthed, jagged public profile can be seen as a rational response to her lived experience. In childhood, the people who should have protected her either abandoned her, ignored her or intimately and repeatedly abused her. The need to scrape a degrading living from an uncaring world with nothing but her teeth and claws to defend herself wasn't likely to soften Aileen's edges.

Aileen is therefore best regarded as a power-oriented serial killer. Intense formative trauma and associated feelings of helplessness may have led to a compulsive need to take back control, with lethal consequences for the men either perpetrating sexual abuse or prompting memories of it. After decades of degradation at the hands of men, it was logical that Aileen was driven to gain and exert power over men, yet utterly tragic that it led not to redemption or catharsis but to yet more tragedy and a death-row reckoning.

ISRAEL KEYES: A FORCE OF NATURE

Imagine a man trained both practically and ideologically from childhood to be a serial killer. Imagine that serial killer conducting his trade with patience and professionalism over a working lifetime, denying law enforcement anything resembling the kind of pattern left by mission-oriented killers or the trail of forensic breadcrumbs left by visionary killers. Imagine a degree of cold, calculating fatalism usually exhibited by veteran soldiers in battle. Imagine a killer who might still be at large, busily and anonymously generating missing-person files, had he not lost his focus and ultimately sought execution.

That killer was Israel Keyes. The three murders that Keyes is positively known to have committed occurred between 2001 and 2012. It is highly likely that Keyes took at least 11 lives in total. He also indulged in kidnap, arson and sexual assault, and committed burglaries and bank robberies to bankroll his murderous vocation.

Israel Keyes was born in 1978 in Richmond, Utah, USA, one of ten children of John Keyes and Heidi Keyes, both committed followers of The Church of Jesus Christ of Latter-day Saints (LDS), otherwise known as Mormons. While John had once been a missionary for the LDS, he would, over time, lead his family towards a cloistered, insular religious vision very far from any mainstream Christian notions of evangelism or altruism. Israel and his siblings were isolated from wider society, homeschooled at first, then led into the wilderness to become skilled extremists.

In the early 1980s, John Keyes abandoned the LDS, embraced a malign, white-supremacist form of Christianity and took his family to a remote area of Washington State, where they lived in a spartan, single-room cabin without basic amenities. Israel was raised in a cult and trained from childhood for religiously ordained race war; indeed, his name was a reference to British Israelism, a warped reading of history that holds that Anglo-Saxons were appointed by God to hold dominion over supposedly inferior races.

The ultimate origins of Keyes's murderous nature remain unclear, but his upbringing actively encouraged and developed skills and traits that would predispose him towards killing and make him rather good at it. Israel Keyes hunted, killed and dressed game for the table of the family cabin, and learned to enjoy both killing and torturing animals. Israel Keyes was often a leader in a tiny sequestered family community and had no rules or boundaries save those he set for himself. From the age of ten, he tested and thrilled himself by breaking into strangers' cabins, stealing and selling guns, stalking animals slowly and patiently for torture and food and setting fires for nothing but the thrill of destruction.

At the age of 14, Israel Keyes hung a living cat from a tree, pierced its belly with the blunt barrel of a handgun and watched on as it thrashed and circled and spewed blood. Also present was another teenage boy, who blanched, vomited and told Israel's parents what he'd seen. While Keyes learned the importance of keeping some of his pleasures to himself, he also learned that frightening those around him was a power he could enjoy and exploit.

Keyes grew up self-contained, self-sufficient and competent in many practical skills. By the age of 16, he'd mastered woodwork sufficiently well to build his family a cabin. As he approached adulthood, he underwent a reverse Damascene conversion, rebelling against his parents' eccentric and life-limiting religious zeal by declaring himself an atheist. Keyes was evicted by his parents, who forbade his siblings from any contact with him. It is of note that he still retained a need for an all-encompassing belief system; rather than simply stepping away from belief altogether, Keyes became fascinated by Satanism and the idea of ritual murder.

As Keyes would reveal to investigators years later, he'd almost made good on his promise to Satan. He claimed that in the summer of either 1997 or 1998, he'd patiently stalked a teenage girl from the wooded banks of the Deschutes River in Maupin, Oregon, then sexually assaulted her with a view to sacrificing her to Satan. Keyes couldn't go through with the killing on that occasion; his timidity was the only part of the crime that appalled him and he resolved it would never stop him again.

In 1998 at the age of 20, Keyes enlisted in the US Army and served as an infantry soldier both inside the USA and in Egypt until he was honourably discharged in 2001. While he was generally well regarded for his fitness and competence, he was an unnerving and sometimes frightening presence to his colleagues, telling at least one that he'd have enjoyed killing them. After military service, he returned to the

Pacific Northwest, starting a family in Neah Bay, Washington State, then in 2007 moved to Alaska, where he established himself as a building contractor and was well regarded for his tradecraft and trustworthiness despite making some of his female clients decidedly ill at ease.

For Israel Keyes, a reputable full-time job in a remote part of the USA was nothing more than cover, a social treeline from which to stalk prey. He took his complete serial-killing playbook to the grave but some things are known. He systematically frustrated investigative profiling by finding multiple, dissimilar types of victim in locations all across the USA and often very far from his home. He planned his killings months in advance and favoured rural, secluded locations. While he was skilled with firearms, he preferred to get hands-on, ideally strangling victims so that he could savour the light fading from their eyes. On his murderous expeditions, he never used his mobile phone, paid for all goods and services with cash and used so-called murder kits cached in remote locations months or years ahead of time.

For reasons that remain unclear, Keyes's mind and methodology began to unravel in February 2012 in the course of his final murder. Samantha Koenig, 18, was kidnapped by Keyes from the coffee booth she ran in Anchorage, Alaska. He stole property including her debit card, tortured and sexually assaulted her and then murdered her the next day. Having stored her remains in his garden shed, he flew with his family to New Orleans, from where he embarked on a two-week cruise. On his return, he tried to make Samantha's remains look alive by applying make-up and stitching her eyes open, photographed her with a copy of a local newspaper from a few days earlier and issued a ransom demand for US$30,000. After a part payment for the ransom was made, Keyes dismembered the body and disposed of it in Matanuska Lake.

Keyes's conduct throughout his last murder and the cynical extortion and theft that flowed from it was uncharacteristically reckless. After the bogus ransom demands had been answered, he travelled to the Southwestern USA and continued to use Samantha Koenig's debit card to withdraw cash. Law enforcement was able to track these withdrawals, gain an idea of what kind of car the suspect was driving and geographically box Keyes in. In March 2012 in Lufkin, Texas, a Texas Highway Patrol officer and a Texas Ranger were on the lookout for out-of-state rental cars when they came across Keyes driving slightly over the speed limit and stopped him.

Keyes was found in possession of Samantha Koenig's mobile phone and debit card, and cash stained with a dye pack from a bank robbery, and was arrested. Under interrogation, Keyes offered to confess only to crimes that he believed investigators would eventually figure out for themselves. He admitted the murder of Samantha Koenig in February 2012 and the double murder of William Currier, 49, and Lorraine Currier, 55, in Essex, Vermont, in June 2011. In the latter case, Keyes had broken into the Currier home at night, bound both of them, driven them to a derelict house, then shot William dead before sexually assaulting and strangling Lorraine to death. Their remains have never been found.

Even then, Keyes's cooperation was contingent on the authorities giving him an execution date and avoiding negative publicity for his family. Investigators couldn't realistically meet either one of these conditions and Keyes withdrew cooperation. Keyes also made a remarkable escape attempt, picking the lock of his handcuffs with discarded wood shavings, only to be subdued with a Taser by marshals.

While imprisoned in Anchorage in December 2012, Keyes managed to acquire a razor blade despite tight security and killed himself by simultaneously cutting his wrists and hanging himself. He took the bulk of his offending history with him, leaving only partial confessions to three murders, hints at others and a cryptic set of drawings that was found in his cell. He had drawn 11 skulls, one pentagram and the words "we are one" in his own blood.

A significant number of other murder victims might have met their ends at Keyes's hands, but this will never be confirmed. Detectives have raised the possibility that at least eight other victims crossed paths with Keyes based on his modus operandi, his movements and hints he made in interviews. One of them was double amputee Special Olympics skier Julie Harris, 12, who disappeared in Colville, Washington State, in March 1996 and whose prosthetic feet were found by the Colville River. Another was Cassandra Emerson, 12, also from Colville, who disappeared in June 1997 after the body of her mother, Marlene Emerson, 29, was found in their burned-out caravan. The deaths of Julie Harris and Cassandra Emerson appear to give the lie to Keyes's self-serving claim that he never targeted children.

Israel Keyes was a clear-cut power-oriented serial killer. Despite the fact that he shared little personal insight with law enforcement before his death, his almost literally spartan upbringing taught him to master and plunder his environment with patience and lethal skill, and inculcated in him a contempt for anyone outside his immediate circle of belief and experience. While he appears to have abandoned his faith in God as an adult, he spent much of his life enacting the harsh lessons learned in the Washington wilderness and from his parents' harsh religious dogmatism.

In *No Country for Old Men* by Cormac McCarthy, the character Anton Chigurh is ostensibly a paid hitman but is in effect and in his own mind an unstoppable force of nature, an agent of death without prejudice and without compunction. He can be seen as a personification of the fear of escalating violent crime, for he is a force that can no more be reasoned with than a tsunami or an earthquake. Israel Keyes was cut from the same cloth, a calm, competent killer whose mind was uncluttered by delusion or fanaticism. It was in his nature to kill, and if you crossed his path then it was in your nature to be killed.

CHRISTOPHER WILDER: THE SNAPSHOT KILLER

For six weeks in early 1984, Christopher Wilder blazed a trail of terror across the USA, abducting 12 women and children in various states and murdering eight of them. He would never face public justice nor share any insight into his motivations, dying by gunshot during a botched arrest attempt.

Christopher Wilder was born in Sydney, Australia, in 1945 to an American father and an Australian mother. While no parental abuse has been reported, he was lucky to survive childhood, nearly dying at birth and almost drowning in a pool while still a toddler. It is known that from late adolescence he associated sex with subterfuge, coercion and violence. In his early teens, he became an active voyeur, trying to peer through windows at women in states of undress. When he was 17 in 1963, he took part in the gang rape of a 13-year-old girl, for which he was sentenced to probation and counselling.

Five years later in 1968, Wilder married, but his wife soon discovered that he had a dark side. A week after the wedding, he was questioned over a series of sexual assaults and his new wife left him and began divorce proceedings. She would later allege that, inter alia, he had tried to kill her and had tried to seduce both her mother and her sister. Wilder's warped sexual appetites might have given rise to imminent criminal sanctions in Australia had he not moved to the USA in 1969. Indeed, flitting from one legal jurisdiction to another might be considered part of his modus operandi and it certainly sustained his offending.

It may also be significant that, on at least one occasion, his parents facilitated this. When he visited them in Australia in 1982, he found time to abduct two teenage girls from a beach and sexually abuse them and was reported to Sydney police. His parents posted his bail and he fled back to the USA pending a trial that was repeatedly postponed until his death allowed him to cheat the justice system altogether. This begs an interesting question: was he abused by his parents or was he overindulged? What part did they play in forming Wilder's character and facilitating his offending? They may, of course, have been disbelieving, blameless or just baffled.

Wilder had moved to Boynton Beach, Florida, USA, in 1969, where he became successful and wealthy in the real-estate business. He had also developed a sideline in photography, both commercially and as a means to find victims. In the early 1970s, he was charged with various sexual offences but never jailed. In one dress rehearsal for his infamous 1980s offences, he convinced a teenage girl that she might win a modelling contract if she posed for photographs; he then drugged her and raped her in his vehicle. In 1977, a psychologist offered the opinion that Wilder could not be considered safe outside an institution. Nonetheless, Wilder successfully bartered his sentence for various charges down to probation and therapy.

Wilder's first known murder victim was 20-year-old Rosario Gonzalez. Wilder was sufficiently wealthy to indulge his love of fast cars both on the road and on the racetrack. Both Rosario and Wilder attended the Miami Grand Prix on 26 February 1984; she was promoting painkillers for a pharmaceutical company and he was racing his Porsche 911. She was seen leaving the event with a man answering Wilder's description and never seen alive again.

On or around 5 March 1984, Wilder killed again. He'd been dating 23-year-old teacher Elizabeth Kenyon and had proposed to her only to be turned down, ostensibly due to their age difference although her parents had seen signs of physical abuse that she had explained away as accidental. Wilder maintained that he hadn't seen her in weeks and Elizabeth's car was found abandoned at Miami Airport; the car had been backed neatly and competently into a parking space, a feat beyond Elizabeth, according to her parents, as she was a remarkably poor driver. Police interviewed Wilder but found insufficient evidence to proceed. The net was closing, however; the police suspected a link between both missing-person cases, and witnesses were found contradicting Wilder's account. On 13 March 1984, he was spooked by a newspaper article explicitly linking him to the disappearance of both Rosario and Elizabeth and fled in what would turn out to be a murderous panic. These young women's remains were never discovered.

After his first two killings in late February and early March 1984, did Wilder realize that his freedom to indulge his appetites would inevitably be curtailed? If so, it appears that he consciously chose to indulge them fully and ferociously while he could. On 18 March 1984, he took 21-year-old

Theresa Ferguson from a shopping mall in Merritt Island, Florida, killed her and left her remains at Canaveral Groves, where they were discovered five days later.

Rosario Gonzalez and Elizabeth Kenyon never got to testify to the cruelties they had suffered, either personally or forensically, for they disappeared without trace. The first to survive Wilder's uninhibited savagery would tell the world a blood-curdling tale. Linda Grover, 19, was abducted from a mall in Tallahassee, Florida, on 20 March 1984 and driven over the state line to Bainbridge, Georgia, while bound and locked in the trunk of Wilder's car. At a motel, Wilder raped and tortured her, blinding her with superglue dried on with a hairdryer and electrocuting her by applying live copper wires to the soles of her feet. Despite this treatment, this brave and desperate girl bolted for the bathroom, locked herself in and screamed so loudly and persistently that other guests began to get curious. Wilder left his victim in the bathroom and fled in his car.

On 21 March 1984, 23-year-old Terry Walden almost had a lucky escape in Beaumont, Texas. Wilder approached her with his favourite gambit, urging her to model for his photography. She may have smelled a rat, as she turned him down. On 23 March, he found her again and didn't take no for an answer; he forced her into his car, raped her, stabbed her to death and threw her remains into a canal. Terry's remains would be found on 26 March, by which time Wilder had struck again. On 25 March, he abducted 21-year-old Suzanne Logan at a mall in Oklahoma City and drove her 290 km (180 mi) to Newton, Kansas, where he subjected her to intimate horror in a motel room. After calmly breakfasting the next morning, he drove Suzanne to a reservoir near Junction City, Kansas, where he stabbed her to death and dumped her body.

By this time, a nationwide manhunt was underway. Within days, the national news media was urging its readers and viewers to be on the lookout for Wilder, and he had earned a place on the FBI's "most wanted" list. On 29 March 1984, Wilder targeted 18-year-old Sheryl Bonaventura in Grand Junction, Colorado, and may have decided to use her as a hostage. It is not clear what kind of relationship he formed with her or how he ensured her cooperation, but both Wilder and Sheryl were seen sharing a meal at a diner in Silverton, Colorado, and told staff they were heading for Las Vegas. On 30 March, they were seen together at a tourist attraction – the Four Corners Monument where Arizona, Colorado, Utah and New Mexico meet – but Sheryl's usefulness to Wilder soon ran its course and he shot and stabbed her to death near Kanab Creek, Utah, on 31 March.

Wilder had been honest about his travel plans. On 1 April 1984, he stalked and abducted Michelle Korfman, 17, from a cover-model competition for *Seventeen* magazine. Her remains weren't found until May and she would be identifiable only by dental records. A number of Wilder's victims were obliged to endure his company and cruelty for days at a time for reasons best known to Wilder. The convenience of having a ready victim at hand was a possibility, as was a warped, sadistic version of companionship. Having a potential hostage may have recommended itself as an insurance policy, but it is more likely that a passive abductee could serve as both camouflage and bait, and the latter was the case with Tina Risico.

On 4 April 1984 in Torrance, California, Wilder set his sights on 16-year-old Tina Risico. He photographed, abducted and physically abused her, then refrained from killing her, believing that she could be of use to him. She was left in no doubt that she'd be tortured and killed if she defied him and was thus forced to help him find fresh victims. Wilder derived sadistic satisfaction from wielding the power of life and death over young women, as well as from physical and intimate acts of cruelty. He also, by extension, enjoyed the power he gave himself to grant or withhold mercy. He was an aficionado of fear and a connoisseur of manipulation. Tina Risico was forced to become Wilder's accomplice and he may well have savoured his power to make her complicit in horror. He sought to systematically corrupt some of his victims fully, body and soul.

Wilder travelled east with Tina, arriving in Merrillville, Indiana, on 10 April 1984. He coerced Tina into helping him abduct another 16-year-old girl, Dawnette Wilt, from a shopping mall. He then subjected Wilt to a long-duration, long-distance ordeal of rape and electrocution while Tina drove his car to New York State via Ohio. Both girls were repeatedly reminded that one or both would die if either tried to escape or raise the alarm. How the girls endured such treatment is hard to imagine, but within days Wilder had reached another crisis point. Having seen Tina's image on the TV news, he panicked and took both girls to a forest clearing near Penn Yan, New York State, with lethal intent, but only after stopping at Niagara Falls first to take some holiday snapshots. He suffocated and stabbed Dawnette and left her for dead, then apparently decided to keep Tina alive a while longer. Remarkably, Dawnette survived, staggered to a road, flagged down a trucker and lived to tell her tale.

Dawnette was lucky, as Wilder returned to the scene shortly afterwards to make sure she was dead. He found her gone, and his descent into reckless, arbitrary spite gathered pace. On 12 April 1984, Wilder took Tina to a mall in Victor, New York State, to find a car with a view to replacing his own. Seeing 33-year-old Beth Dodge near an eye-catching, gold-coloured Pontiac Firebird, Wilder forced her into his car and had Tina follow him in Beth's car. He took Beth to a gravel pit, executed her with a handgun, dumped her remains and his car there and travelled with Tina to Logan Airport in Boston, Massachusetts. There, he gave her a plane ticket to Los Angeles and cash for a taxi and set her free with instructions to write a book about her time with him. So traumatized was Tina that she didn't make herself known to law enforcement until she arrived in California.

Wilder's race was nearly run. On 13 April 1984, he tried and failed to abduct a 19-year-old woman at gunpoint in Beverly, Massachusetts, then fled towards Canada knowing that the authorities would soon be able to pinpoint him. Later that day, Wilder stopped for directions at a service station in Colebrook, New Hampshire, and found himself being approached by two curious state troopers. He tried to arm himself and one of the troopers tried to restrain him; in the scuffle, Wilder fatally shot himself twice, one of the bullets passing through him and seriously wounding the trooper.

Christopher Wilder is generally considered a power-oriented serial killer. He was also a rapist and an ephebophile, favouring female victims midway between adolescence and adulthood. He was addicted to increasingly grotesque and violent forms of sexual gratification, chasing more intense and taboo thrills up to and including physical and psychological sadism. He may also have been adept and calculating in his manipulation of the judicial system, his victims and his parents. Ultimately, only the power to mete out death and pain at whim would offer the thrills he sought.

Wilder would never face justice nor share his secrets with the world. The remains of some of his known victims have never been recovered, and he may well have killed a dozen more women and girls both in the USA and in Australia. What is clear is that Wilder's power-oriented pathology entailed a remarkable degree of regard for his own squalid appetites. He rejoiced in making the FBI's "most wanted" list and in the thought that Tina Risico might become his awestruck biographer.

It is noteworthy that Wilder owned a well-thumbed copy of *The Collector* by John Fowles, a 1963 novel centred on a disturbed young man who kidnaps the object of his obsession and ultimately steals her life. The book can be read as a chilling critique of a killer's capacity for absurd, egocentric self-justification, but that hasn't prevented it being a favourite of several serial killers – including Wilder, Robert Berdella, Leonard Lake and Charles Chi-Tat Ng – whose own absurd egocentricity ensured that they missed the point altogether.

The only scintilla of justice to be found in this case is this: Wilder's personal estate, valued at US$7,000,000 (equivalent to approximately £21,000,000 in 2024), did not pass to his family but was instead divided up by court order among the families of his victims.

ALBERT DeSALVO: THE BOSTON STRANGLER

Albert DeSalvo makes an unusually ambiguous case for inclusion in this rogues' gallery of serial killers. Ostensibly, he was the man who murdered up to 13 women in Boston, Massachusetts, USA, between June 1962 and January 1964, laying claim to the nickname the Boston Strangler. Doubt, however, remains as to whether he actually committed all, or any, of these murders. What is certain is that the Boston Strangler inspired an unprecedented degree of public fear, due to the post-war boom in mass media. Scaremongering news was no longer limited to newspapers and radio; in the USA of the 1960s, frightening true-crime stories were piped into each and every home in graphic detail via the novel yet suddenly affordable television.

Albert DeSalvo was born in Chelsea, Massachusetts, in 1931. His childhood was blighted by the extreme, sadistic depravity of his father, Frank DeSalvo. Frank abused his wife, Charlotte, on one occasion making his six children watch as he knocked every tooth from her jaw and individually broke every one of her fingers. On multiple occasions, he assembled the whole family to watch as he was pleasured by sex workers.

The extent to which extreme cruelty became a normal part of family life for Albert DeSalvo is debatable, but he did exhibit certain forms of behaviour that are often precursors for serial violence. Before adolescence he indulged in zoosadism and by the age of 12 he had been arrested for assault and robbery. Despite a juvenile criminal record featuring numerous offences of violence and theft, he joined the US Army as a young adult, served with the Military Police and was honourably discharged after two tours of duty. In civilian life, and at the time of the Boston Strangler murders, DeSalvo lived in Malden, a suburb of Boston.

Between 14 June 1962 and 4 January 1964, 13 women were murdered in Boston. While all of these killings were attributed to the so-called Boston Strangler by thrill-seeking news media, and ultimately by law enforcement, the lack of a consistent victim profile and modus operandi was at odds with the usual behaviour of an individual serial killer. While each victim was an adult female, their ages ranged from 19 to 85. Most, but not all, were sexually assaulted and strangled to death with items of their own clothing. One was badly beaten and then stabbed, while another was stabbed without being beaten. One, the oldest, died when her heart failed. All were murdered in their own homes, having been persuaded to grant entry to their killer.

DeSalvo's history of offending hadn't stopped in his teens but did take a few odd turns in adult life. In early 1961, a number of women in the Boston area contacted police to report what would become known as the Measuring Man sex offences. A well-turned-out man had knocked on their doors, told them they'd been selected as potential models for swimwear or gowns, took their hip, bust and other measurements with a tape measure, then left with a promise that someone would be in touch. There had been no theft or violence; if it had been criminal at all, then it was at worst trespass with a diffident sexual assault and a dash of voyeurism.

In March 1961 of that year, DeSalvo was caught by police trying to break into a home in Cambridge, Massachusetts. He confessed to being the Measuring Man and was tried. DeSalvo told Boston police that he'd staged the Measuring Man charade because, as an uneducated, plain-looking man in reduced circumstances, he'd felt the need to put a few clever, middle-class people in their place. He was convicted but a plea in mitigation, based on the fact that he was the sole breadwinner for his family, together with good behaviour meant that he was released in early 1962, a few months before the Boston Strangler murders began.

In 1964, faced with an unprecedented level of public fear and media scrutiny, the Boston Police Department was under pressure. They were, however, set to receive an unlikely boon. A man wearing green overalls, and thus dubbed the Green Man, had committed a series of rapes in Connecticut. On 27 October 1964, a man posing persuasively as a police detective gained entry to the home of a young woman in East Cambridge. He tied her to the bed, raped her, untied her, offered his apologies and left. That victim's description led to several rape victims being shown DeSalvo's photograph and identifying him as their assailant.

DeSalvo was arrested for the Green Man rapes but was not initially suspected of the Boston Strangler murders. After being charged with the rapes, however, DeSalvo offered police a confession to the murders. He was convicted and sentenced to life imprisonment in 1967, but the drama was far from over. He promptly escaped with two other detainees from a secure psychiatric facility, having left a note complaining about the unsatisfactory conditions. He turned himself in days later and was transferred to a maximum-security prison, where he recanted his murder confessions. In November 1973, DeSalvo was stabbed to death in a prison infirmary, allegedly for selling amphetamines below the price mandated by organized criminals in the prison system.

Debate continues as to whether DeSalvo could have been the Boston Strangler. Advances in forensic analysis led to official verification of only one of his claims. DNA analysis proved that he had raped and murdered 19-year-old Mary Sullivan, the final Boston Strangler victim, on 4 January 1964. DeSalvo's remains had been disinterred specifically so that he could give his final testimony in the form of a post-mortem DNA sample. To date, no physical evidence has emerged to link DeSalvo with any other murder.

DeSalvo's proven offending history suggests he had a knack for persuading female householders to grant him entry. That aside, the variation in the modi operandi and victim profiles of the Boston Strangler killings raised the possibility of multiple offenders. Writers and experts continue to cast doubt on the reliability of the forensic evidence tying DeSalvo to Mary Sullivan, although the District Attorney's Department of Suffolk County, Massachusetts, regards it as definitive and, to date, is sticking to its guns.

DeSalvo may have taken the ultimate truth of the matter to the grave. Whether or not he was the Boston Strangler, by convincingly laying claim to that title he made himself the first celebrity serial killer of the post-war, mass-media age. DeSalvo was a power-oriented killer; such offenders seek power to compensate for a perceived helplessness at a formative stage, and they do so by finding ways to manipulate and control others. Sometimes that controlling behaviour manifests as torture and murder. Sometimes, perhaps, controlling a narrative and putting a bunch of supposedly clever people in their place will suffice.

DENNIS NILSEN:
TABLEAUX À MORT

In the late nineteenth and early twentieth centuries, the tableau vivant ("living scene" in French) made a comeback. This medieval art form uses living actors to recreate important or powerful moments from history or drama and freeze them in time. In the pioneering years of photography, it was an entertaining way of creating intricate conversation starters. For restless theatre audiences – and still, occasionally, in modern movies, for those with sharp eyes – the cast would occasionally freeze in position before carrying on with the action. One infamous Scottish serial killer would subvert the medium, murdering the players in his private dramas and thus turning tableaux vivants into *tableaux à mort* ("scenes of death") for his own private pleasure.

Between December 1978 and January 1983, Dennis Nilsen murdered at least 12 men and children in London, UK. He committed all of his known murders at two addresses in North London and was known in British newspapers as "the Muswell Hill Murderer". Paraphilia was at the heart of his killings, in his case an obsession with creating aesthetically pleasing scenes from the remains of his victims, then engaging with them sexually. He is also notorious for disposing of his victims' dismembered body parts via the lavatory; a drain blocked by flesh and bone ultimately led to to his arrest.

Dennis Nilsen was born in Fraserburgh, Scotland, in 1945, one of three children of Elizabeth Whyte and Olav Moksheim, a couple brought together by the Second World War. Moksheim, who adopted the surname Nilsen, was a soldier of the Free Norwegian Forces who escaped the Nazi occupation of his homeland. Elizabeth and Olav married in haste in 1942 and repented at leisure; he was diffident towards the marriage and often absent and the couple divorced in 1948.

Nilsen would later characterize his childhood as contented, but there were nonetheless formative heartbreaks. He idolized his grandfather, who may have served as a father figure, and counted the days when he was away at sea working in the fishing industry. The old man was unwell, however, and died at sea when Nilsen was five years old. As was traditional, the deceased lay in an open coffin in the Whyte family home prior to burial, and despite his tender years Nilsen was obliged to look upon the cadaver. This made a significant and possibly defining impression on the boy: he saw somebody he revered in a still, ornate and dignified tableau, and was repeatedly reassured that his grandfather was sleeping and was at peace.

It can't have helped Nilsen's developing psyche that he grieved quietly and for far too long over his grandfather, spending much time away from home staring at the comings and goings of the local fishing boats and building up resentment towards his happier siblings. Another formative event occurred when Nilsen was eight or nine years old. While on a solitary walk along the beach at Inverallochy, he strayed beyond the tideline and was submerged beneath the water, where he would have drowned had a passerby not dragged him out. Not only had he retained a fascination with the sight of the dead in peaceful, waxen repose, but he got close enough to drowning to experience the acceptance of death. The peace that followed and magically erased the initial flailing panic represented a kind of ecstasy and would feature in his killings.

To compound Nilsen's disaffection with his family and wider society, he realized in adolescence that he was gay. In an age when homosexuality was both socially taboo and criminalized – consenting sexual relations between same-sex partners wasn't decriminalized in the UK until 1967 – being gay could be a source of confusion, unhappiness and fear. It is emphatically not the case that there is a straight line to be drawn from being gay to becoming a serial killer; many struggled with their sexuality without being drawn to the darkness that so captivated Nilsen. In Nilsen's case, the feelings of shame and estrangement that flowed from being gay in that era were just one part of a complex web of mental health issues and happenstance.

From the age of 14, Nilsen began to take steps to escape rural Scotland, joining the Army Cadet Force with a view to later signing up for military service. Two years later, in 1961, Nilsen joined the Army Catering Corps and spent 11 years in the military, completing his service with the rank of corporal in 1972. He engaged with military life enthusiastically and seems to have particularly appreciated the chance to travel and expand his horizons. He became more convinced of his sexual orientation but took care to hide it from his comrades. He also learned to drink heavily, a time-honoured, off-duty pastime in the British military. This gave rise to another tableau that would feed his murderous imagination. While stationed in former West Germany in 1964, Nilsen woke up on the floor of a German youth's dwelling unsure about how he'd got there. While he hadn't been intimate with the youth, the scenario inspired a recurrent fantasy that would later become lethal reality; at the heart of it was the idea of a slender youth being sexually used while unconscious and thereby wholly passive.

Nilsen also became acquainted with violence, and perhaps more confident in his ability to deploy it. During a posting to Aden (now Yemen) in 1967, he was kidnapped by a local taxi driver who knocked him out and locked him in the trunk of the car. When the car stopped and the driver dragged him out, Nilsen seized the tyre jack, beat the man insensible and locked him in the trunk. While in Aden, Nilsen remained unable to express his sexuality with other men and made do with increasingly elaborate fantasies. These fantasies incorporated both the idea of the slender, helpless youth and his own encounters with death and violence.

To fulfil his imaginary scenarios, Nilsen would try to split his consciousness and thereby alternate between the roles of abuser and victim; he may have become adept at the dissociation required to kill without compunction. He also incorporated a famous work of art into his fantasies. The 1819 painting *The Raft of the Medusa* by Théodore Géricault is a vivid depiction of a real nautical disaster in which 135 of 150 sailors set adrift in the Atlantic died of starvation and dehydration, while 15 survived by cannibalism. Detailed in the lower left of the painting is a pale, recumbent, helpless and naked youth, lying atop a dismembered body and being dominated by a muscular and cruel older man.

POWER-ORIENTED SERIAL KILLERS

In Cyprus in 1969, Nilsen forced himself to try sex with a female sex worker and, despite the fact that he bragged about it often and emphatically, privately found it unsatisfactory. After leaving the military in 1972, he temporarily stayed with his family in Scotland. A TV documentary provoked an argument: Nilsen spoke up for gay rights, while his brother mocked him and told his mother that Dennis was gay. Nilsen left for London soon after and became almost entirely estranged from his family.

During 1973, Nilsen joined the Metropolitan Police but resigned when he received an inheritance from his father. He also had a number of liaisons with men he met in gay bars but found that casual sex brought only doubt and frustration. In 1974, Nilsen joined the UK's civil service and would work in job centres, finding employment for unskilled labourers, until his arrest in 1983. Between 1975 and 1978, Nilsen became convinced that, while he craved a stable, fulfilling sexual relationship, he was incapable of making one work. He had one long-term relationship that lasted from November 1975 to May 1977, but it ended in mutual acrimony and resentment having proved ultimately unequal, loveless and sexless.

If Nilsen had learned anything about himself, it was that he was self-sufficient with very specific physical needs. In 1978, he set about finding an answer to these needs and did so with a consistent modus operandi. He sought out victims who were sometimes gay and sometimes straight, sometimes homeless and sometimes not; what mattered was that they exhibited a need that could be exploited. He would find them in pubs, on buses and trains or in the street. They would be tempted into Nilsen's home by the offer of company, alcohol and perhaps a bed for the night. Once they were relaxed and at ease, Nilsen would strangle them to death, typically with a ligature. If they were unconscious but still breathing, Nilsen would drown them by holding their heads underwater in a bath, sink or bucket. When he began his killing in 1978, Nilsen was living alone in a spacious ground-floor apartment at 195 Melrose Avenue, Willesden Green, London. Significantly, that property gave him access to a void beneath the ground floor and a garden.

Nilsen took his time with grooming his victims and then handling their remains. They would be cleaned in a ritual manner so that the feel and appearance of their lifeless bodies could be appreciated. They would typically be dressed and then stored in Nilsen's home, sometimes for weeks, so that they could be aesthetically appreciated and physically abused again. Finally, they would be dismembered and disposed of, either by burning on outdoor bonfires or by having their flesh and bones sectioned into small parts and flushed down the lavatory. Nilsen later confessed that, while he had pleasured himself over several of his own *tableaux à mort*, he had never penetrated his victims. His murders followed a strict aesthetic code.

Nilsen's first victim was 14-year-old Stephen Holmes. On 30 December 1978, Nilsen had been whiling away a lonely Christmas week with solitary drinking. On an impulse, he decided that he had to leave his home and find somebody to talk to. Nilsen went to a local pub, where he saw the underage Stephen trying and failing to buy alcohol. He persuaded Stephen to join him at home with the promise of free booze. At Nilsen's apartment, both he and Stephen listened to music and drank until they passed out. Nilsen woke the next morning to find Stephen asleep beside him on his bed. He decided that Stephen should keep him company until the end of the holidays and wasn't prepared to risk his saying no. He strangled him with a tie while he was still sleepy and disoriented, drowned him with a bucket, washed his body, placed him carefully on the bed and performed sex acts. He then stored the body beneath his floorboards until August 1979, when he removed it and burned it in the garden.

Nilsen would repeat this modus operandi many times despite an early encounter with the police. On 11 October 1979, he met Hong Kong student Andrew Ho in a pub and enticed him back to his apartment with the promise of sex. Nilsen then botched his attempt to strangle Ho, who fled and reported the incident. Police officers interviewed Nilsen but Ho declined to support a charge and no prosecution was forthcoming.

Despite his close encounter with law enforcement, Nilsen couldn't resist his new compulsion. On 3 December 1979, he met Canadian tourist Kenneth Ockenden, 23, in a pub and offered to show him the sights. The tour ended with free hospitality and fatal strangulation at Nilsen's apartment, and Kenneth's body was kept and repeatedly abused. On 17 May 1980, Nilsen struck up a conversation with 16-year-old Martyn Duffey, a student who'd been sleeping rough for several days and was therefore highly receptive to an offer of free food and accommodation. Duffey too was throttled and drowned and his body kept and abused.

The pace of Nilsen's killings increased markedly after the murder of Martyn Duffey, suggesting that he was now completely in thrall to his murderous compulsion.

The majority of those he killed in 1980 have not been identified but did nonetheless present him with a very specific problem: putrescence. By late 1980, the various bodies secreted beneath the floorboards were decaying and stinking and both attracted and hosted a variety of insect life. In a ghoulish episode that must have challenged even Nilsen's paraphiliac tastes, he removed a number of bodies seething with maggots and emanating a foetid, unendurable stench of corruption, dissected them and burned them on a bonfire on abandoned ground near his home. He finished by raking and smashing any obviously human bones, including at least one complete skull. It may say something about the nature of urban life that neither the miasma of decaying life nor the swarms of flies or the public burning of human remains seem to have attracted any inconvenient attention for Nilsen at that time.

Nilsen appears to have spent Christmas 1980 alone but the New Year didn't bring a new start. From January to April 1981, Nilsen claimed at least another four victims, sticking to his modus operandi with callous regularity. His final victim at 195 Melrose Avenue was 23-year-old Malcolm Barlow, strangled in his sleep in September 1981 after calling in to thank Nilsen for helping him get medical attention a day or two earlier. Soon afterwards, Nilsen was compelled to remove and burn evidence and then relocate so that his landlord could renovate the property. Whether his landlord ever got rid of the smell of rotting flesh is not known.

Nilsen moved to an attic apartment at 23 Cranley Gardens, Muswell Hill, and seems to have stayed his hand for several months. This may be because he now lacked easy access to underfloor storage and a garden, making the logistics of murder and paraphilia trickier. He is known to have resumed his killing in earnest in March 1982, but was nearly hoist by his own petard. Lured to Nilsen's home by the promise of a free drinking session, 23-year-old John Howlett woke up to find himself being strangled and responded in kind. While Howlett succumbed and was eventually drowned, Nilsen was shaken and went to work with his latest victim's fingermarks visible on his neck.

In May 1982, Nilsen may have had a crisis of conscience. He found 21-year-old Carl Stottor in a gay pub in Camden, drowning his sorrows following a relationship breakdown. Nilsen persuaded Carl to join him for drinks and commiseration at his apartment, plied him with more alcohol, then repeatedly tried and failed to kill him. Over several days, Carl floated in and out of consciousness and was variously throttled, half drowned and resuscitated. Eventually, Nilsen told Carl he'd choked himself in the fastening of a sleeping bag while sleeping and had been immersed in water as a cure for shock. Carl was escorted to a train station and sent on his way, baffled but luckier than he knew. Why Nilsen spared Carl remains open to speculation. It is known that Nilsen was a heavy drinker, and his recollection of his victims would later turn out to be patchy. Circumstances suggest that Nilsen may have been somewhat sober and thus more open to remorse when he noticed that the young man was still alive. The ultimate truth remains moot.

In June 1982, Nilsen strangled 27-year-old Graham Allen, kept him in his bath for three days, then called in sick so that he could dissect the body in the kitchen. Nilsen claimed his final victim, 20-year-old Stephen Sinclair, in January 1983. By this point in his killing career, Nilsen had perfected his routine. He cleansed Stephen's body, applied talcum powder to accentuate its paleness, placed it on his bed, then arranged mirrors so that he could see himself lying tenderly with the dead man. He subsequently dismembered and dissected the body, placing some parts in bin bags bound with the very bandages that Stephen had used to conceal scars on his wrists from suicide attempts.

In February 1983, in a moment of black farce, Nilsen wrote to his landlord to complain that the drains were blocked and creating an intolerable stench. He may also have been exhibiting a dissociative mental state. A commercial drain cleaner attended the address and instantly discovered that the main drain was jammed with small bones and a foul, gelatinous, flesh-like substance. Nilsen was one of the residents who discussed the problem with the drain cleaner, and allegedly wondered aloud whether someone had been flushing fried chicken down the lavatory. When the cleaning company returned the next day, they found that the main drain had been cleaned overnight. Suspicious, they explored further and discovered more of the foul matter in the pipe that led to Nilsen's attic apartment.

The police were called and some of the bones and flesh were analyzed by a pathologist. They confirmed that the remains were human and that one piece of bone came from a neck and bore a groove from a ligature. Detectives visited Nilsen, who granted them entry to his apartment. They blanched at the unmistakable stench of putrefying flesh and, when challenged, Nilsen told the officers where they could find the remaining body parts. He added that he wanted to tell them the whole story but it would take time, so perhaps the police station would be a better venue.

Nilsen promptly gave detectives a full and frank confession. If it lacked detail in places, it was only because he hadn't known very much about many of his victims. He would also return with police to the scenes of his crimes to assist with the recovery of body parts. When pressed on what had motivated him, he replied that he was hoping somebody might explain it to him. He was tried for six murders and two attempted murders in October 1983. Other victims would not be identified until much later, and some never would be.

Psychiatrists for Nilsen's defence team claimed that he suffered, inter alia, from a lack of emotional development, narcissistic personality disorder, an ability to depersonalize others and a tendency to use others as inanimate proxies for his own gratification. Their contention that he was not guilty of murder by reason of diminished responsibility failed to convince the jury and Nilsen was convicted as charged. He received a whole-life term and died in 2018 at the age of 72.

Nilsen is usually regarded as a power-oriented serial killer and is thus unusual in that he didn't suffer serious abuse or deprivation as a child. He did, however, suffer childhood unhappiness and insecurity that became associated with specific concepts and images that evolved into templates for murderous sexual fantasies.

A Latin phrase, "*ars gratia artis*", means "art for the sake of art". The phrase was popularized in the nineteenth century by artists and bohemians who held that art doesn't need to improve public morals or teach wholesome lessons to justify itself. It can be amoral or subversive and still succeed if it expresses some deeper truth. In the depths of his dissociative, murderous egocentrism, Dennis Nilsen had his own artistic vision. The fact that so many cruel, lonely deaths, and the reduction of humans to filth and corruption at his hands, didn't dissuade him from this vision should make the reader think deep and troubling thoughts.

TED BUNDY: CONTROLLING THE NARRATIVE

"The loveliest trick of the Devil is to persuade you that he does not exist!" So wrote Charles Baudelaire in 1864, although the idea has been restated in fiction several times, most memorably in Bryan Singer's 1995 crime thriller, *The Usual Suspects*. If the reader has yet to see that movie, consider this a spoiler alert. The key conceit of *The Usual Suspects* is that both the audience and the lead detective are duped into believing the murderer's version of events. Much of the movie is told in flashback as "Verbal" Kint, a small-time crook only tangentially involved with serious criminals, grudgingly trickles out his story to a tough cop. At the end, however, we find out that Kint is in fact a fearsome master criminal, Keyser Söze, who has been flexing his muscles by deceiving both the cop and the audience. He vanishes like smoke in the breeze and remains legendary for his cruelty, his showmanship and his powers of manipulation.

Ted Bundy is thought to have kidnapped, raped and murdered dozens of women and children during the 1970s in various states of the USA. Bundy was the quintessential power-oriented serial killer, principally because of his powers of manipulation. As a high-functioning psychopath, he would form the template for many fictional imitators. In Bundy's case, psychopathy endowed him with an almost total absence of empathy and conscience accompanied by a determination to exploit others by superficial charm and emotional manipulation. Psychopathy falls within the contemporary definition of antisocial behaviour disorder, and in Bundy's case was accompanied by sadism and paraphilia.

Bundy was born Theodore Cowell in 1946 in Vermont, USA. As an infant, he was initially cared for by his maternal grandparents, Samuel Cowell and Eleanor Longstreet, in Philadelphia. In 1950, Bundy's mother, Eleanor Cowell, took her son to live with cousins on the opposite side of the USA in Tacoma, Washington. Various reports of Bundy's childhood have emerged, but the fact that many came from Bundy himself means they should be taken with a generous pinch of salt. For example, he alleged that his grandfather abused his spouse and animals and was vocally racist, while his grandmother was timid and clinically depressed, but these allegations are disputed.

It is known that Bundy harboured a lifelong animus against his mother for not identifying his real father. While growing up in Tacoma, he supposedly became estranged from his new family and cultivated a vivid and dark inner life, fantasizing about naked and dead women, and about leading a life of importance and influence. He is alleged to have enjoyed inflicting cruelty on stray cats and other children in the neighbourhood. On one occasion, this involved setting punji traps – sharpened stakes set in covered holes in the ground – one of which caused serious injury to a child.

Bundy claimed to have had a solitary adolescence, because he couldn't understand how relationships worked. Despite the fact that he was an intelligent, diligent student who graduated from high school and went on to university, he broke the law when it suited him. When he turned 18 and his juvenile criminal record was expunged, he'd committed multiple instances of burglary and car theft. He also stole equipment and forged lift passes so that he could pursue his hobby of skiing.

If it is true that Bundy initially struggled to understand and build social relationships – and this would be consistent with psychopathy – then he learned to fake it well enough to appear conventionally sociable and successful. In 1967, he began a long-term romance with a fellow student, Diane Edwards, whom he later claimed had been his only true love. In 1968 at the age of 21, he dropped out of education and, between dead-end jobs, volunteered in political campaigns, including a stint as bodyguard and driver for Arthur Fletcher, a Republican politician who pioneered affirmative action. Later that year, Diane ended her relationship with Bundy, frustrated by his immaturity and fickleness.

His separation from Diane Edwards proved a crisis for Bundy and provoked a period of soul-searching with far-reaching consequences. He drifted across the USA, continued his college studies in a sporadic, ad hoc way, and developed a taste for violent sexual expression, initially in pornographic form. In late 1969, Bundy returned to the Pacific Northwest and began a relationship with Elizabeth Kloepfer that would endure throughout his years of prolific killing. He became stepfather to Molly Kloepfer when she was three and remained in her life until she was ten. She would later allege that he'd subjected her to occasional violence and sexual assault, presenting his behaviour as playful and harmless.

To the outside world and to the women in his life, Bundy appeared to find focus. He completed a college degree in psychology and may well have gained insights into his own pathology and the tactics and techniques that would later be used by law enforcement and court psychiatrists against him. He resumed his interest in political campaigning and became a streetwise and resourceful aide to the local Republican Party. In 1973, while still committed to Elizabeth Kloepfer, he resumed his relationship with Diane Edwards, who'd been amazed at his transition from dropout to budding political player. When Bundy cut all contact with Diane in early 1974, she eventually understood that he had been taking a specific form of revenge on her: he wanted her to feel the rejection he felt she had inflicted on him.

She was lucky. In the spring of 1974, Bundy dropped out of law school. While it appeared that he'd given up on yet another career, he had in fact embraced his true vocation: serial killer. Bundy was prolific, highly organized and careful as a killer. He would later brag that he had mastered crime-scene hygiene early in his career, and the gross mismatch between murders conclusively and inconclusively linked to him seems to bear this out. It is also of note that killers like Bundy would almost certainly have been identified earlier had twenty-first-century DNA profiling been available.

In the public consciousness, Ted Bundy is often associated with a specific vehicle, his light-brown Volkswagen Beetle. Beginning with the movie *The Love Bug* in 1969, the Beetle appeared on the big screen in a series of Disney movies as Herbie, a big-eyed car with an adorable personality. The

Beetle, alongside the Volkswagen Bus, also came to be associated with the counterculture movement of the 1960s and 1970s, and by extension with vague notions of peace and love. There is thus a perverse logic in Bundy using the cute, innocuous Beetle as camouflage that allowed him to stalk, approach and kidnap many of his murder victims.

In Bundy's typical modus operandi, he presented himself as harmless, either suffering a physical impairment or representing law enforcement. Victims would be persuaded into his Beetle, where they would be beaten unconscious, handcuffed and then driven away. They would later be raped and murdered and then abused in multiple ways post-mortem. He sometimes indulged in necrophilia until organic decay made it impossible, and kept a number of severed heads as souvenirs. While he preferred to offend in widely dispersed and secluded outdoor locations, he did occasionally invade homes to rape and murder.

Bundy conducted a campaign of horror against young women in Washington and Oregon during the first six months of 1974. A few survived, like 18-year-old Karen Sparks. In January, around the time that Bundy jilted Diane Edwards, Bundy beat Karen around the head with a length of metal from her bed frame and then violated her with it so viciously that he damaged her internal organs. She survived with permanent brain damage. Many young women suffered unknown but equally cruel treatment and were then dispatched and disappeared. From January to June, one female student was disappearing every month.

Young women who had near misses with Bundy would confirm his modus operandi. In April 1974, after 18-year-old Susan Rancourt disappeared in Ellensburg, other students reported being approached by a man wearing an arm sling who asked for help to carry a stack of books to his Beetle. By June, local and federal law enforcement knew that they had a serious problem and were beginning to devote significant resources to the investigation. Bundy was neither impressed nor deterred. In the early hours of 11 June, Bundy persuaded 18-year-old student Georgann Hawkins to follow him to his Beetle. He bludgeoned her with a crowbar, handcuffed her, drove her 32 km (20 mi) away, raped her, strangled her and spent the night abusing her body. In the meantime, a major crime-scene investigation had got underway at the scene of the kidnap. Realizing he'd left Georgann's earrings and one shoe at that scene, Bundy returned and managed to retrieve them from under the noses of numerous police officers.

Bundy had chutzpah and a dark sense of humour. Even as witnesses came forward with descriptions of a solicitous young man on crutches with a leg in plaster and a brown Beetle, he was settling into his new job, advising women how to protect themselves from rape for a crime-prevention initiative. The police investigation remained stymied for want of forensic evidence and on 13 July 1974 Bundy added insult to injury. On a bright, sunny day at a crowded beauty spot in King County, Washington, he kidnapped two young women, drove them away and murdered them. Three women had lucky escapes when they were approached by Bundy, smelled a rat and got away. At least the police had enough survivor testimony for a good artist's impression of the suspect, and public broadcast of it led to Bundy being put forward as a suspect. In an echo of the Yorkshire Ripper inquiry in the UK, however, the police were overwhelmed by the volume of information being generated and initially discarded Bundy simply because he was an educated, outwardly decent man with no criminal record, his juvenile history having been expunged.

In August 1974, Bundy moved to Salt Lake City, leaving a cold trail of unexplained disappearances and murders in Washington and Oregon and beginning a new killing spree in Utah. Again, insult was added to injury for law enforcement: one of Bundy's victims was 17-year-old Melissa Smith, daughter of a local police chief. Melissa was kidnapped from a Salt Lake City suburb and, when her remains were discovered in the wilderness nine days later, the pathologist estimated that she had endured seven days of unimaginable cruelty before she was killed.

Bundy kept up a relentless tempo of kidnap, rape, torture and murder in Utah, but one young woman had a lucky escape. On 8 November 1974, he persuaded 18-year-old Carol DaRonch into his Beetle by pretending to be a police officer. She noticed that Bundy wasn't driving towards the police station and he panicked, pulled over and accidentally applied both handcuff bracelets to the same wrist, allowing her to make good her escape. Later the same day, a key left at the scene of the kidnap of 17-year-old Debra Kent was found to fit the handcuffs that had been taken from Carol DaRonch.

Soon afterwards, Bundy returned to Seattle and to Elizabeth Kloepfer. He didn't tell her about the various other women he'd been dating, or about the greater number he'd been torturing and killing, and she didn't tell him that she'd reported him to King County law enforcement as a murder suspect multiple times. Remarkably, the relationship endured and plans were made for her to visit him in Utah. In early 1975, Bundy resumed his life in Utah but began travelling into Colorado to stalk and murder women. On 12 January,

23-year-old Caryn Campbell was kidnapped from inside her shared dwelling in Snowmass Village and her brutalized remains were discovered weeks later. Numerous other young women would share her fate that year.

In the meantime, however, investigators in Washington State were getting creative. Complex criminal enquiries today benefit from computer technology; pulling meaningful patterns out of vast tranches of data without bespoke computer technology was remarkably difficult, a point made clear by the stories of Ted Bundy, Peter Sutcliffe and other killers of the pre-digital age. All that was available to those hunting Bundy in Washington State was the King County payroll computer. In August 1975, they found a way of inputting lists into this huge, primitive, proto-computer and outputting correlations. When criteria ranging from Volkswagen ownership to social circles were input, Bundy's was one of a limited number of names that kept popping out.

Around the same time, Bundy was stopped and arrested in his car in Salt Lake City. He had been prowling a suburb in the early hours and had tried to flee a highway patrol officer. The front seat of his Beetle had been removed and Bundy was in possession of a comprehensive murder kit including a ski mask, handcuffs, rope, plastic bags and a crowbar. Despite a search of his apartment, there was insufficient evidence for a charge and Bundy was released and placed under surveillance. The dots were being joined and Utah detectives travelled to Seattle to speak to Elizabeth Kloepfer. She declined to give Bundy an alibi for various dates and times when young women were known to have been taken and confided to them various suggestive details of her life with him. He mysteriously kept stolen crutches and plaster of Paris in Elizabeth's home, for one example. For another, he became distressed when she talked about cutting her hair; it transpired that her usual hairstyle matched that of Bundy's preferred victims.

In September 1975, Bundy sold his Beetle and law enforcement seized it, stripped it for evidence and found hair samples matching Caryn Campbell, Melissa Smith and Carol DaRonch. In October, Carol identified Bundy in a line-up and there was finally a meaningful offence with which he could be charged. Remarkably, Bundy's mother and stepfather paid US$15,000 (approximately US$122,000 in 2024) to bail him out. For months, police officers in Seattle expended considerable resources in keeping Bundy under constant surveillance while multiple teams struggled to find the hard evidence needed to end his killing career.

Bundy was convicted of attempting to kidnap Carol DaRonch in early 1976 and sent to Utah State Prison. In October, he was interrupted in an escape attempt and spent months in solitary confinement. In June 1977, he was extradited to Aspen, Colorado, to stand trial for the kidnap and murder of Caryn Campbell. Ever the manipulator, schemer and performer, Bundy chose to speak in his own defence and was thus not obliged to wear handcuffs or leg shackles. While supposedly researching case law in the court library, he jumped from a second-floor window and made good his escape. He lived rough and stole food, weaponry and a car, and remained at large for six days until police officers detained him again.

With the trial set to resume, Bundy's compulsive drive to break rules and manipulate the game were set to fatally undermine his own best interest: hubris set up a date with nemesis. The prosecution case was falling apart and depended heavily on evidence that was ruled inadmissible. Bundy was advised to weather the storm, watch the current case fail, serve the 18-month remainder of his earlier conviction and walk away scot-free. Instead, he persuaded friends and supporters to smuggle in a floor plan of the jail and cash, and he procured a hacksaw blade from other inmates. He patiently sawed a hole in his cell's ceiling, explored the crawl space, waited until the Christmas holidays when many staff were absent, then broke out of the jail having passed through the quarters of the chief jailer and stolen his clothes. By the time the escape was discovered 17 hours later, Bundy was 1,900 km (1,200 mi) away in Chicago.

After escaping from jail in Colorado, Bundy found his way to Florida, where he stole to support himself and unleashed hell on more unfortunate young women. In what may have been his most notorious act, in a period of no more than 15 minutes in the early hours of 15 January 1978, he entered a sorority house in Tallahassee, murdered two young women and attempted to murder two more. He severely assaulted another young woman and murdered a 14-year-old girl before he was arrested for the final time. Three lives were lost and three more ruined as a result of poor jail security in Colorado. On 12 February 1978, a Florida police officer stopped a stolen Volkswagen Beetle near the Alabama state line. At the wheel was Bundy, who kicked the officer to the ground and ran. Bundy was chased down and subdued after a life-or-death struggle for the officer's handgun.

Nemesis would keep its date with hubris. Bundy was tried for his Florida murders in Miami-Dade County in June 1979 and once again, and against all legal advice, represented himself. Such was his arrogance that he declined a plea deal that would have taken execution off the table. Remaining in control mattered so much to the arch-manipulator that Bundy dispensed with the legal expertise that might have saved his life. Despite a bravura display of spite, arrogance, delusion and other courtroom theatrics, Bundy failed to impress Florida's jurors and received three death sentences.

The manipulative games Bundy played with investigators suggest that he enjoyed selectively sharing and withholding details of his crimes so intensely that it amounted to another form of post-mortem abuse. He told one psychologist that he had claimed two victims in New Jersey in 1969. He told another interviewer that he'd made his first kill in Seattle in 1971. He hinted that he'd killed in Washington State in 1972 and 1973 but would say no more. It may be that the entirety of Bundy's life of crime, from adolescence to execution, was one sustained act of manipulation. His life story is strewn with hints as to what made him so obsessed with the cruel exercise of power, but a manipulator of his calibre rarely confided anything unless he could gain some spiteful victory by doing so. Trying to catch the truth of Ted Bundy's origins and motivations is like trying to catch smoke. He was executed by electrocution in January 1989.

ANDREI CHIKATILO: THE RED RIPPER

In ancient Jewish folklore, the golem is an anthropomorphic being created from base matter by mystic ritual in order to protect the community from whose earth it sprang. In modern use, the figure of the golem has acquired a more flexible identity and can be male or female, and good or evil, but is usually a crude, sinister imitation of humanity albeit with supernatural origins.

One of the most memorable news images of 1992 showed Soviet-Ukrainian serial killer Andrei Chikatilo on trial in Rostov-on-Don in south-western Russia. He lurked behind bars, shaven-headed, swivel-eyed and gape-mouthed, a golem of evil and a caricature of humanity, raised from the earth to drag dozens of victims down into its cold, muddy embrace. Powerful as that image is, however, it belies the truth. Chikatilo may well have sprung from a cursed land and carved out a story worthy of the darkest passages of the Old Testament, but he thrived as a killer because in his prime he looked like everyone's favourite uncle.

Between 1978 and 1990, Andrei Chikatilo sexually abused, murdered and mutilated a minimum of 52 women and children in Russia, Ukraine and Uzbekistan, all part of the USSR in that time period. He was convicted and sentenced to death by a Russian court in 1992 and executed by a single bullet to the head in 1994. By the standards of his childhood, however, he'd had a reasonable life and a tolerable death. Chikatilo was born in Yabluchne in the Ukrainian Soviet Socialist Republic (SSR) in 1936 to desperate farm labourers who lived below the poverty threshold, worked the land unpaid and lived in a single room. His childhood was blighted by the cruelty of two of history's most homicidal dictators.

Chikatilo grew up in the aftermath of the Holodomor, a famine caused by radical and rapid reforms to agriculture and industry mandated by Joseph Stalin and which resulted in at least 3.5 million deaths by starvation in the Ukrainian SSR. It is widely accepted that this famine was weaponized by Stalin to undermine Ukrainian nationalism and amounted to genocide. Growing up a few years after the Holodomor, Chikatilo's childhood was still blighted by hunger, poverty and fear of starvation. Eating leaves and grass was not unusual and he claimed that he hadn't tasted bread until after the Second World War.

Chikatilo was also haunted by a family story of the Holodomor. He never knew his older brother, Stepan, because the boy had been stolen away, butchered and eaten by desperate neighbours. The truth of the story could not be verified but it was not inconceivable during the dark days when the starving had lain down on the streets of towns and villages to die. In 1941, Chikatilo turned five and had to reconcile himself to yet another form of horror. Adolf Hitler had launched his invasion of the USSR, a war explicitly aimed at subjugating or exterminating the Slavic peoples and acquiring their land. Until German forces were expelled from his homeland in 1944, Chikatilo's formative experiences included hiding in cellars and ditches while bombs fell, civilians and soldiers were arbitrarily executed, and buildings – including on one occasion his own home – were razed to the ground.

Chikatilo's father was absent for the whole of this period, having been conscripted to the Red Army in 1941, and Andrei shared the family's single bed with his mother. To compound his fear and anxiety, he remained prone to bed-wetting beyond infancy and was beaten for it. As if there weren't already enough horror and degradation in this family saga, the birth of Andrei's sister, Tatyana, in 1943 may well have been the result of rape by a passing German soldier; both the rape and the consequent birth may have occurred in the same family bed. It is of note that such rapes were a routine and widespread feature of the war between the USSR and Nazi Germany.

Despite his appalling childhood, Chikatilo rallied in adult life, superficially at least. As a teenager and young man, he was an able student and a passionate party activist, and he completed his military service with a spotless record. His sexuality, however, was a matter of perpetual dysfunction, distress and worse. At the age of 17, he sexually assaulted an 11-year-old girl but had ejaculated before he could subdue or rape her. Later, relationships with adult women foundered due to anxiety and self-consciousness so extreme that he was rendered impotent. Remarkably, he had two children in the 1960s, both conceived without intercourse.

In the 1970s, Chikatilo worked as a teacher, but was too timid and diffident to maintain order in the classroom. He also developed a reputation for voyeurism and sexual touching directed at the teenagers in his charge. Nonetheless, he stuck at teaching, combining it with his vices, which ultimately escalated. On 22 December 1978, he committed his first known murder. He lured nine-year-old Yelena Zakotnova to a hut he had purchased for the purpose in Shakhty near Rostov-on-Don, tried and failed to rape her, then achieved sexual release as he stabbed her to death. Chikatilo learned a lesson that he would embrace: he could achieve orgasm only by stabbing women or girls to death, and he ardently wanted to repeat the experience.

While Chikatilo wouldn't face justice for the murder of Yelena Zakotnova until 1994, he wasn't the only one who would be executed for her death. In a parable of Soviet-era justice, where extreme confirmation bias was the norm, a labourer with previous convictions for rape and murder, Aleksandr Kravchenko, was selected as the suspect by the authorities despite the fact that there was no physical evidence connecting him and he had a good alibi. By contrast, eyewitness accounts and a blood trail linked Chikatilo to the victim and the crime scene. Nonetheless, Kravchenko's wife was coerced into recanting her alibi evidence and he was forced to confess and later executed.

In 1981, Chikatilo lost another teaching job following more complaints of child molestation. He moved on and became a *tolkach*, an operative who helped to game Soviet productivity figures by travelling between industrial centres to trade commodities and favours. This gave Chikatilo the time and latitude to indulge his budding appetites across the USSR. Having learned to appreciate the nature and power of his compulsion, and perhaps having understood the lucky escape afforded him by the fate of Aleksandr Kravchenko, Chikatilo embarked upon his long and appalling career of murder with a characteristic modus operandi.

Typically, Chikatilo targeted lonely and vulnerable young people unlikely to be missed, ideally homeless, involved in sex work or addicted to substances. He favoured bus or rail termini because they fitted in with his working life and because the constant churn of anonymous people made him practically invisible. Intended victims were lured to secluded or wooded areas with food or drink, then savagely attacked. He gouged out victims' eyes with such ferocity that eye sockets were striated by blade strikes. He appears to have physically enacted his intense shame by blinding those whose eyes saw his true self, even in death. Sexual organs were often attacked out of spite, with females defeminized and occasional male victims castrated. Sometimes he cut off and chewed the flesh of his victims, owning them entirely and indulging in a fantasy that he was a war hero who had captured and given the enemy their just deserts.

For 12 years, Chikatilo hid in plain sight, riding the rails across the USSR and sating his appetites whenever the opportunity emerged. The USSR's internal security system delivered a significant number of confessions to his crimes by taking both known sex offenders and vulnerable young men with intellectual disabilities and beating and berating them until they admitted whatever they were told to admit. Nevertheless, the killings continued, despite the fact that Chikatilo's luck almost ran out in September 1984. He was observed stalking and attempting to molest young women by undercover detectives at a bus station, arrested and found to be in possession of a large knife, several ropes and a quantity of lubricant. A fluke of clinical sampling would come to

Chikatilo's rescue: his blood was found to be type A, whereas crime-scene semen samples had been classified as type AB. He served a short prison sentence for an unrelated offence of theft and was then free to resume his killing.

The defining image of Chikatilo from his 1992 trial is at odds with how he appeared during his killing career. He approached his victims as a polite, well-spoken, well-turned-out middle-aged man. Although his briefcase carried the means of murder, he exploited Soviet-era egalitarianism and its respect for elders and may well have been automatically addressed as "uncle" by those he approached. This chimed with the personality profile compiled for Soviet law enforcement by a psychiatrist in 1985, the first time such a measure had been taken in a Soviet-era serial-killer enquiry. Dr Alexander Bukhanovsky suggested that the killer was a man between 45 and 50 years old who had endured a traumatic childhood and an adult lifetime of sexual impotence. The act of murderous penetration with a knife was the suspect's proxy for the sexual intercourse of which he was incapable.

By 1990, bodies were still being found with appalling regularity. Glasnost had also arrived and with it a more free and less deferential press keen to draw the public's attention to the numerous murders and to apply pressure to public officials. The killer's pattern was analyzed and a plan hatched to trap him. The biggest rail stations would be so saturated with uniformed police officers that the killer would be bound to favour smaller stations that were covertly saturated with plain-clothes officers. All officers were ordered to stop, question and note the details of any man seen with a young woman or child.

On 6 November 1990, Chikatilo lured 22-year-old Svetlana Korostik away from Donleskhoz station near Shakhty and murdered her in woodland. On his return to the station, an undercover officer noticed that Chikatilo had muddy, grass-stained knees and elbows and blood on his face and hands and was attempting to wash himself at a well. He was also wearing a business suit and was not equipped for mushroom-picking or rambling. The officer stopped Chikatilo, recorded his details, let him go and filed his report. When Svetlana's body was discovered two days later, Chikatilo was identified as a likely suspect and the threads began to be drawn together. His previous business employers were able to correlate his known movements with a number of murders, and various schools confirmed his sexual misdemeanours.

Chikatilo was placed under surveillance and on 20 November 1990 was arrested while trying to lure children to a park with beer. He initially denied any knowledge of the crimes, despite the kill kit found in his possession and the defensive human bite mark in his finger. He was also obliged to provide samples of both blood and semen, clarifying a critical point of confusion in the forensic evidence. While Chikatilo's blood and saliva showed as blood type A, his semen showed as type AB. This explained why a type-A blood sample taken from him in 1984 had failed to correlate with numerous type-AB crime-scene semen samples. On 29 November, Dr Bukhanovsky read to Chikatilo from his long psychological profile, prompting a tearful shock of recognition and a full and detailed confession.

Andrei Chikatilo was a power-oriented serial killer. His childhood delivered a toxic mixture of familial claustrophobia and social isolation and exposed him to sustained hunger and the risk of lethal violence. It also normalized pain, suffering and physical degradation and taught him that he had no power to resist or hide from these cruel primal forces. Flowing from this and compounding it were social awkwardness and sexual impotence, all manifesting in a rapacious desire to find a substitute for sexual release through extreme violence and thereby exert the power that had been denied him. It may have been a legacy of the Holodomor and its cultural hangover that Chikatilo's warped sexual release was intertwined with mutilating and consuming human flesh.

Chikatilo was tried and executed, and his story endlessly analyzed, as the Cold War ended, the USSR fragmented and a new and uncertain future began to unfurl. Looking at the broken figure in that 1992 courtroom with a degree of historical awareness, it was as if the land itself had been stained by innumerable acts of cruelty and bloodshed and spawned a golem driven to visit that cruelty on innocent victims. Innocence is, alas, no defence against history or serial killers, but when has it ever been?

TOMMY LYNN SELLS: THE C2C KILLER

According to the US Federal Highway Administration, the USA is criss-crossed by almost four million miles of roadway. This tally includes multi-lane highways and gridlocked city streets, but it mostly consists of three million miles of rural roads. Crossing the USA's voluminous interior by car or bus will acquaint the traveller with a seemingly endless and often lonely set of landscapes, from wide-open prairies to parched deserts, and from jagged, tree-fringed mountains to monotonous fields of corn. Whether they are a driver or a passenger, such a traveller might feel lonely and untethered, just a speck in an indifferent and uncaring vastness. If they happen to glimpse missing-person reports on the morning news or the side of milk cartons, or read about the exploits of serial killers, they might wonder just how many poor souls have been plucked from these millions of miles of roads, and the ragged settlements that cling to them, and swallowed up by the landscape.

If any serial killer personifies that frisson of roadside horror, it is Tommy Lynn Sells. While he was convicted of only one murder, it is generally accepted that he killed at least 22 victims between 1979 and 1999 and he himself claimed more than 70. He was a truly itinerant serial murderer, drifting from state to state throughout a 20-year time span, rootless, ruthless, killing seemingly randomly and earning himself the nickname the Coast-to-Coast Killer, or C2C.

Sells was born in Oakland, California, in 1964, one of five siblings, to a single mother. He and his twin sister, Tammy Jean, contracted meningitis when they were 18 months old; she died and he somehow survived. His mostly absent father died in Tommy Lynn's childhood and he was cared for negligently or not at all by his mother. It is claimed that he developed alcohol dependency from the age of seven, around the time that he was being regularly sexually assaulted by a local man with his mother's connivance. By the age of ten, Sells was abusing both alcohol and drugs. At the age of 13, he climbed into his grandmother's bed, possibly with sexual intent, and was evicted and abandoned by his family. He shot a stranger out of pure, impersonal rage – they fortunately survived – then left town to begin living the life of a nomad.

Sells was a power-oriented serial killer, following a tragically familiar pattern. The gross neglect and harm visited upon him in his formative years formed a template by which he would seek to assert control over those who crossed his path. Indeed, he later claimed he'd been reliving childhood abuse while abusing others. Sells lived a homeless, itinerant life of utter misery between 1978 and 1999, travelling thousands of miles by hitchhiking and train-hopping. The cruelty he inflicted was as savage as it was impersonal.

On one instructive occasion in May 1992, 19-year-old Fabienne Witherspoon saw Sells begging in Charleston, West Virginia, and resolved to help. She invited him to her home and asked him to wait outside while she prepared food for him. He allowed himself in and attempted to rape her at knifepoint. She fought back desperately, getting control of the knife and seriously wounding him. He responded by beating her around the head with a piece of furniture. Had Sells not been so badly hurt that he ended up in intensive care, then the story might have ended differently. As it was, he was jailed for five years and diagnosed with bipolar disorder.

Bipolar disorder was only one of Sells's many problems. During an 18-month prison term for vehicle theft in Wyoming, he was diagnosed with personality disorder with antisocial and schizoid features accompanied by psychosis as well as depression and a persistent dependence on both drugs and alcohol. Aside from a handful of years spent in prison, Sells spent nearly two decades inflicting his psychiatric trauma on innocents all over the USA.

Sells lost his liberty for the final time due to the courage of a survivor. On 31 December 1999 near Del Rio, Texas, he attacked two children. He sexually assaulted and fatally cut the throat of 13-year-old Kaylene Harris, then inflicted a similar wound on ten-year-old Krystal Surles. Remarkably and despite a severed trachea, Krystal got herself to a neighbour's home almost 0.5 km (0.25 mi) away and gave such an accurate description of Sells that he was detained soon afterwards. He was convicted of murdering Kaylene Harris and sentenced to death.

At the agonizing heart of the story of Tommy Lynn Sells is the lack of decisive closure his chaotic confessions afforded the families of his many victims. This was compounded by the fact that Texas forbade death-row inmates from leaving the state, even for the purposes of assisting other jurisdictions with murder enquiries.

Numerous detectives spent thousands of hours listening to Sells's confessions and worked hard to distinguish fact from fantasy. Sometimes he confessed to bona fide crimes but related the circumstances incorrectly or inconsistently, obliging prosecutors to disregard him. Sometimes, he confessed to crimes that simply couldn't be shown to have happened at all.

The only rays of light in this litany sprang from two exonerations. Joel Kirkpatrick, ten, was murdered in Lawrenceville, Illinois, in October 1997; the boy's mother, Julie Rea-Harper, had been convicted of the crime but was exonerated when Sells's confession decisively corroborated her version of events. JoAnne Tate, 35, was murdered in St Louis, Missouri, in April 1982; her daughter, Mellisa DeBoer, came to believe Sells had killed JoAnne, and the suspect she'd erroneously identified when she was a seven-year-old child was released.

Detectives eventually realized that, consistent with his cruel, controlling pathology, Sells used his confessions as a way of exerting control and manipulating the justice system. However, he has been linked by sufficiently detailed confessions together with independent corroboration to 22 murders, including the killing of Kaylene Harris, which led to his final arrest. The first crime on this list was the fatal shooting of John Cade, 39, in Port Gibson, Mississippi, during a home invasion in July 1979. The penultimate crime was the abduction, rape and murder of Bobbie Wofford, 14, in Kingfisher, Oklahoma, in July 1999.

Sells lacked a precise modus operandi, but many of his crimes featured vengeful and indiscriminate savagery against a variety of strangers – men, women, teenagers and young children – against whom he could have had no rational, personal animus. Their geographical distribution was also consistent with Sells's lifestyle of constant travel and occasional unskilled work. In July 1985, to take one example, he met 28-year-old Ena Cordt and her four-year-old son Rory Cordt while he was working at a carnival in Springfield, Missouri. He went home with them, was discovered stealing by Ena, beat her to death with a baseball bat, then dispatched Rory in the same manner as he was a witness. To take another, in October 1987, 21-year-old Stefanie Stroh disappeared while hitchhiking near Lovelock, Nevada. Sells strangled her to death, covered her in concrete and dumped her in a hot spring to make sure that she could never be located or recovered.

Sells was an archetypal power-oriented serial killer, in thrall to a murderous spite that burned so brightly it didn't need a cause, an ideology, a pretext or otherworldly voices as kindling. Sells's grim life was a zero-sum game: he won a succession of victories by taking everything from at least 22 people. That this pathology is ultimately nihilistic, leading to violent death not for any cause but for its own sake and nothing more, should chill us all.

Sells was executed by lethal injection in Huntsville, Texas, on 3 April 2014. He declined to make a final statement. The unnerving possibility remains that of the numerous rambling, inconsistent, unverifiable murder confessions made by Sells, which did not make it on to a list of confirmed cases, some were truthful. There is also the possibility that he kept many killings to himself or perhaps simply forgot about them or conflated them with others while in thrall to drink, drugs and psychosis. In either case, there may still be many missing people whose remains lie undiscovered in wild, desolate places, perhaps within shouting distance of one of the millions of miles of highway along which a killer passed on his way to death row.

FINAL WORD

Whether a crime storyteller is writing a screenplay, a novel, a social media post, a podcast or a news article, they need to grab your attention and keep you glued to the page or screen or earbuds until the bitter end. These storytellers generally stay within touching distance of the truth, but a sober appreciation of reality comes a poor second to the need to shock, disturb or terrify.

If you have been shocked or unnerved by these stories of modern history's most notorious serial killers, you should bear in mind that, while they appeal to storytellers for obvious reasons, your chances of crossing the path of such a monster are remote. The *Global Study on Homicide 2023* published by the UNODC offers a more nuanced picture of global murder patterns, based on figures from 2021.

Of 458,000 individuals murdered globally in 2021, 81 per cent were male. Where you live matters: per 100,000, the Americas had a homicide rate of 15, followed by Africa with 12.7, Oceania with 2.9, Asia with 2.3 and Europe with 2.2. Most at risk in the Americas were males aged 15 to 29, who accounted for 53.6 per cent of victims. Your region also affects how you're likely to be killed: in the Americas, 67 per cent of homicides featured firearms compared to 12 per cent in Europe.

Globally, 31 per cent of victims were killed by intimate partners or family members. In Europe, this goes up to 69 per cent. Organized crime accounts for 50 per cent of homicides in the Americas but only six per cent in Europe. Homicide caused more deaths in 2021 than war or terrorism, and two distinct patterns emerged: while more than eight in ten homicide victims were male, lethal violence in the home skewed towards women, who accounted for 66 per cent of all intimate-partner murders.

Serial killers are rare enough to be statistically insignificant by these metrics. It is also cause for celebration that global homicide rates are trending slowly downwards. But risks still exist, and the vast, complex warp and weft of abnormal psychology, multigenerational abuse, social deprivation and pure bad luck will keep producing broken people prone to violence. So, don't have nightmares, but do keep your eyes wide open.

SERIAL KILLERS

Shocking True Stories of the World's Most Barbaric Murderers

JAMIE KING

SERIAL KILLERS

Shocking True Stories of the World's
Most Barbaric Murderers

JAMIE KING

ISBN: 978-1-83799-122-8

Maybe it's because our animal instincts draw us to dangerous situations; maybe it's because reading about predators allows us to learn about their behaviours in a safe setting. Whatever the reason, serial killers and their crimes have fascinated us for centuries.

This true crime compendium not only relates the disturbing events that transpired but also delves into the psychology of the perpetrators. The stories within are shocking and often difficult to comprehend, but with this deep dive into the world of the macabre, readers may gain a greater understanding of the motivations and thought processes of these murderers.

This book is a must-read for anyone interested in the psychology of crime and the human mind.

TRUE CRIME STORIES

STORIES

Shocking Tales of Real-Life Murderers, Thieves, Con Artists and Gangsters

JAMIE KING

TRUE CRIME STORIES

Shocking Tales of Real-Life Murderers,
Thieves, Con Artists and Gangsters

JAMIE KING

ISBN: 978-1-83799-007-8

Prepare yourself for the urge to sleep with the light on, because these stories are not for the faint-hearted. With stories of criminal activity that span across the world, this book will take you on a journey to the darkest reaches of human nature, including:

- The true events that inspired the horror film *Friday the 13th*
- The people behind the cyber attack that cost over £90 million in damages
- The Roman poisoner who became the world's first known serial killer
- The carpenter who was executed by electrocution for kidnapping and murder

Whether you're a true crime junkie or just morbidly curious, let these stories of charismatic criminals and their sinister deeds ensnare your interest and send a shiver down your spine.

Have you enjoyed this book?
If so, find us on Facebook at **Summersdale Publishers**, on
Twitter/X at **@Summersdale** and on Instagram, TikTok and
Bluesky at **@summersdalebooks** and get in touch.
We'd love to hear from you!

www.summersdale.com

Image Credits